TCHEHOV, THE MAN

By the same author:

THE AGE OF CANDLELIGHT

PORTRAITS OF GENIUS

ANTON TCHEHOV
1860 — 1904

BEATRICE SAUNDERS

TCHEHOV, THE MAN

LONDON
CENTAUR PRESS
1960

© Beatrice Saunders 1960

Published by

Centaur Press Ltd., 11-14 Stanhope Mews West, London, S.W.7

Printed in Great Britain by
The West Yorkshire Printing Company Limited, Wakefield.

Contents

Introduction

WHAT a relief it is to know that the day of "debunking" in biography has passed! For, surely, there was too much of it. It is so easy to destroy, to tear a man to tatters, to impute ignoble motives to all his actions. Shakespeare has said that "The evil that men do lives after them; the good is oft interred with their bones". That may be true, but so far as I am concerned, this will not happen with Tchehov, for if ever a man's nobility of soul was apparent it was in this man. Inevitably he was aware, from early manhood, of exceptional literary talent, yet this was used, for the most part, for the furtherance of the Russian cause (although he was no revolutionary) and for the assistance of his family. For most of his life he gave himself to literature as almost a holy cause, and finally he sacrificed to it both health and happiness. His philanthropic work for Russia (at that time a very backward country) in the building of schools and roads, etc. was a very real contribution, his medical work was a service to humanity, and his altruistic work in the convict island of Sahalin was a noble effort. Like all great artists he was an extremely sensitive man, yet to the end of his life he carried himself with dignity and humility. He was not a saint, but his life and character were so wholly admirable that it would be difficult to overpraise him. I therefore make no apology for writing this life in the only way that was possible. To me he has always been an inspiration, and I regard it as an honour to write this book.

Chapter 1

Boyhood

O N February 19th, 1861, by a decree of the Tsar, the emancipation of the serfs in Russia finally became law, and 22,500,000 human beings were released from the bonds of serfdom. This event, the most prodigious social revolution accomplished in Europe since the French Revolution, was of profound significance, not only as a symbolical act, but because it changed the whole social structure of Russia.

It is true that before the emancipation many serfs were perfectly happy; they had been born in slavery and therefore had no thought of following any wishes but those of their masters. Yet other serfs were treated with extreme cruelty, and it was not unusual for a man to be given a thousand strokes of the rod. Indeed, it is recorded by the aristocratic Turgenev that in his mother's household a serf-girl who picked a tulip in a hothouse was almost beaten to death, and a peasant was made to walk forty-five miles in order to bring a pot of buckwheat from a distant farm. Stewards and overseers (serfs themselves) were often particularly cruel to their subordinates. Young girls, too—if they were good-looking—were casually used as mistresses by the sons or masters of the house, and any children born of such unions merely became additional serfs in the large household.

The Russian lord and large landowner, before the emancipation, was served and lived like a king, and his menage can only be compared to a large household of the Middle Ages in England. Hundreds of servants ministered to the needs, whims, passions and amusements of himself and his family. In addition to relatives, adopted children and hangers-on, there were innumerable valets, nurses, footmen, coachmen, postilions, housemaids, cooks, scullions, table-deckers, couriers, stove heaters, stable-boys, cellar-men, lamp-lighters, and gardeners. There was a band of musicians, also a family doctor; and there were hosts of tutors, teachers, governesses (German, French and Russian), female companions, stewards, etc. The lower grades of servants were regarded almost as animals, and their masters neither knew nor cared where they slept; they could doss on the hay, in a barn or shed, or even sleep with the cattle in the fields.

Although it was possible for a serf to purchase his freedom, very few men could achieve this high ambition. The money had to be laboriously earned and saved, rouble by rouble, for many years; the price of freedom was a high one. Yet it is recorded that at least one man succeeded in doing this very thing. The grandfather of Anton Pavlovitch Tchehov, born in slavery, did by persevering labour, buy back the freedom of himself and his family, twenty years before the abolition of serfdom, for the sum of 3,500 roubles. It was an event which had a profound influence for life on the author, for the fact that his grandfather had been a serf was never forgotten. Anton had been taught from birth to accede always to the wishes of his superiors, to kiss the priest's hand, and to be thankful for every small blessing sent from God. Indeed, he confessed later that it was many years before he was able to "squeeze the slave out of himself, drop by drop".

The shackles of slavery had also left their mark on Anton's father, and he would flop to the ground before a bishop, bow reverently to every carriage which passed him on the road, and prostrate himself when he said his prayers. He crossed himself twenty times a day, kept all the fasts religiously, and could not pass a church or the picture of a saint without murmuring a prayer. Like the majority of Russian peasants he was superstitious, and a fatalist. When misfortunes came he would murmur resignedly "It is the will of God", and even as the tears streamed from his eyes he would say "It was ordained".

Anton Pavlovitch Tchehov was born in Taganrog, Southern Russia, on January 17th, 1860, and was the third son of Pavel Egorovitch Tchehov, and his charming, gentle wife, Yevgenia Yakovlevna, the daughter of a Taganrog cloth merchant. As a girl she had travelled all over Russia with her father in the course of his business, and she had had a fairly good education; this was unusual, as nine-tenths of the population in Russia at that time were illiterate. The family consisted of five sons and one daughter—Alexander, Ivan, Nicolay, Anton, Michael and Marie. Their father was in many ways an unusual man, for although he kept a small grocer's shop he was an excellent musician and a good violinist; in his spare time he painted ikons. He also took an active part in the affairs of the town and held the post of choirmaster in the Taganrog Church, a task he fulfilled with almost fanatical enthusiasm. He was a handsome man, with his elegant pointed beard and very fine eyes, but he was vain and selfish, and it is clear that he disliked his trade; he felt that such an occupation was degrading. Surely he was too cultured a man to have to wear a grocer's apron and spend his days handing out soap and candles. Such paltry merchandise! His soul was filled with music—the exquisite ecclesiastical music composed by the monks of the middle ages, and to descend from those glorious heights to the bare and cold reality of a humble shop made him shudder with distaste. His customers were, for the most part, poor and even ragged. They depressed him, for were they not a continual reminder of the slavery in which he had been born? He had endeavoured to raise himself, but poverty and the cares and needs of a large family had dragged him down. He loathed the shop; whenever possible, therefore, he made his sons deputise for him.

Young Anton would be sent behind the counter almost before it was light (shops opened very early in those days) and with cuffs and threats would be set to work. "Learn the business. Learn the business!" his father would shout irritably, and if things went wrong Anton was whipped.

How the boy detested the shop, for on a winter's morning the cold was intense, draughts blew in all directions, and his icy fingers shook so much that he could barely tie the apron round his threadbare coat. Every limb would be aching with cold, and there was a pain at his heart that was almost unbearable; he was numb all over and could not count the change, yet his father would pull him by the ear and cuff him on the head. Was this the reputed happiness of childhood? There was no time to read, to go tobogganing in the snow—like other children—to visit friends, or to play games. Indeed, Anton remembered the shop with loathing and bitterness all his life. "In my childhood I had no childhood" he said.

But the grocer's fanaticism for his religion caused even more unhappiness in the Tchehov household, as the moment school was over innumerable sacred duties had to be performed with the most scrupulous fidelity. From earliest infancy the children were given strict religious instruction, and were taught zealously to observe all the fasts; they were trained to assist at the altar and to ring the church bells. Choir practice took place almost every night, and would often last until midnight, as the earnest and excitable choir-master demanded an extremely high standard. First he would solemnly strike a note with the tuning fork, and then he would make them repeat their chants, anthems and hymns over and over again. The young trebles would strain their boyish voices in an effort to please him, but he would frown, bite his lips and grow purple with anger. Raising his baton in a frenzy he would shout hoarsely "Piano! . . . piano! . . . More lightly . . . more lightly." Then at the appropriate moment he would roar "Let yourselves go . . . Glory! Basses . . . G-L-O-R-Y . . ." At last, red, perspiring and exhausted, he would sit down, and the choir broke up. Then the boys would stagger up to bed, almost too tired to undress.

On great Feast days, when the morning Mass had to be sung, the boys would be wakened by their father at two or three in the morning and marched to church. Religious processions, too, took up endless time. As choristers they had to follow the banners and the ikons, they had to watch the priest and the sacristan with a vigilant eye, and above all they had to *sing*. If they forgot the words or sang out of tune they would be sharply punished.

Neighbours protested that it was wrong and cruel to deprive growing boys of necessary sleep and rest, but the grocer would retort "At Mount Athos the boy chanters sing for nights on end. I myself have sung from my early childhood and thank God I am strong. To work for God is never harmful." Indeed, he was immensely proud when his boys were old enough to sing "The Archangel's Voice" in church, and the trio "May my prayer be exalted". But the young choristers, as Anton confessed later, felt like "little galley slaves".

There can be no doubt that Anton's gentle mother did not approve of her husband's harshness, but like the majority of Russian women of her class, she was a dutiful and obedient wife. Her family was a large one, and her burden was heavy. When she was worried she would steal away for a few moments to cross herself and gaze reverently at the ikons, where the small lamp burned night and day. "God is good" she would say, and she would pray that the Heavenly Mother would guard and preserve her children. When they came to her at night for her blessing she would make the sign of the cross over them. "My dove! My little soul!" she would say tenderly, as she noticed Anton's pale face (the Russian language is rich in endearments); "You are tired. Go to bed and sleep; here is your candle."

But the shop was not the only place where life was difficult and exacting for Anton; he was frequently sent into the country to stay with his grandfather, who was in the service of Count Platov. Here the boy was made to assist with the threshing. He had to sit all day, often from dawn till dark, to write down the number of poods and pounds of threshed corn. The steam engine whistled, hissed, creaked and boomed "Like the sound of a whistling top", and clouds of dust rose as the lazy oxen trod. How painfully the hours dragged! How interminable the day seemed! The whole scene, in fact, was stamped on his memory for the rest of his life—the grimy, perspiring faces of some three-score men working in deadly earnest. Nor while staying with his grandfather was Anton ever allowed to forget that he was the grandson of a serf. When his superiors passed, he was taught to stand respectfully aside and bow to the ground. He was taught to be self-effacing, obsequious, and to speak only when addressed.

Anton was sent first to be educated, at the age of seven, to the parish school in Taganrog, where the head-master, a coarse, ill-educated Greek, thrashed the children frequently. The boy's companions were chiefly the children of artisans, sailors and labourers. But at the age of nine he was transferred to Taganrog High School, where he made excellent progress. Books were his passion, and he soon evinced a strong urge to write; there were sketches for the school magazine, composed in a remarkably mature and concise style. But Anton was also an excellent mimic and actor, with a sense of humour which simply bubbled over. He much enjoyed writing and producing plays of his own. He and his brothers also organized amateur performances of various well-known plays. These took place in the large drawing-room of the house of one of Anton's friends. The Tchehovs, in fact, were passionately fond of the theatre, and whenever Anton had a rouble to spare he rushed to the gallery of the local play-house. As time passed, too, he began to take a keen interest in birds, and he became the possessor of a few pigeons and a dovecote. The bird-market had a tremendous fascination for him, and his tall, slim figure was often to be seen there, accompanied by two black dogs, his inseparable companions.

In the meantime, tragedy was gradually overtaking the Tchehov household, for the grocer, who had never been seriously interested in his business, had allowed his affairs to become hopelessly involved, and day after day he sank deeper into debt. Taganrog, it is true, had lost its importance as a port and trading centre since the railway to Vladikavkaz

Tchehov reading *The Seagull* to the Moscow Art Theatre Group
(On Tchehov's right is Stanislavsky and next to him Olga Knipper, the leading lady, whom Tchehov married)

had been built, but that alone could not account for the grocer's failure. He had let matters slide, and then, borrowing left and right, he had lost his head. Finally he could pay neither his dues to the Merchant Guild, nor his loan or interest to the bank, and Anton would return from school to find his mother in tears and his father walking excitedly up and down, scolding, explaining, protesting. Life was cruel, the fates were unkind, ill-luck was his portion he declared, and throwing up his hands, he would groan and roll his eyes.

But finally the crash came, and as debtors in those days were sent to prison, there was no alternative for Pavel Egorovitch but to fly to Moscow; in that large city he would be able to hide and eventually find work. His two elder sons were there already, as Alexander was studying physics and mathematics at Moscow University, and Nicholay was attending the Moscow School of Painting, Sculpture and Architecture.

It was a mournful departure, this skulking away of the head of the family, yet for his wife, now penniless and alone, worse was to come, as the house and shop in Monastery Street were sold by auction and one of the creditors took all the furniture. Whether friends or relatives came temporarily to their assistance is not recorded; all that is known is that the grocer's wife soon followed her husband, taking with her the youngest children, Marie and Michael. But Anton, who wished to finish his education at the High School, remained; he had courageously decided that he could support himself by tutoring.

The parting between the boy of sixteen and his family was a heart-breaking one, and for some months he was wretchedly unhappy. The struggle with poverty, too, was unceasing, as tutoring was badly paid, and he could only visit pupils after school hours. Nor was it easy to find enough pupils. Indeed, these were dark and difficult days. Lonely and hungry, he would trudge through the snow for miles (he was too poor to afford goloshes), and on his return home after a difficult teaching session he was obliged to study for his own examinations. That he was able to support himself was remarkable, yet apparently he succeeded, and was also able at times to send money to his parents. They were having a desperate struggle against poverty and were quite unable to assist him. They were living in a dark basement in Moscow, in the very poorest quarter of the city, and were obliged to sleep on the floor, covered by blankets and overcoats. They could not afford to buy fuel, and had to change their quarters continually— ostensibly to avoid creditors. Anton's father had been unable to find work, and his absurd escapades were merely an added burden. Nevertheless, he still strutted about as master of the house, and pinned a set of rules on the wall, in which he set out the duties of each member of the family.

To Anton, alone in Taganrog, the letters from Moscow were piteously sad. For what would become of them all? Would they die there of starvation, or would they resort to begging in the streets? . . . Night after night he lay awake tortured by anxiety . . . Yet life must go on, and fortunately he had some friends in Taganrog. There was, in particular, a charming Polish family with daughters, to whom he was much attached. They were keenly interested in music, and had shewn him much kindness. Occasionally, also, he was asked to dine with his rich relatives, who were glad to entertain this intelligent and handsome youth, with the delightful manners and clever wit. But on such occasions Anton was painfully conscious of his shabby clothes. He was extremely sensitive, though courage and a natural dignity compelled him to hide the fact. Sometimes, too, when an evening party had been particularly pleasant and a pretty girl had lingered as she pressed his hand in farewell, he would be forced to remind himself grimly that nothing must deflect him from the path of duty; he had too many commitments. Love, gaiety and freedom were not for him. "I love every kind of merry-making," he confessed at this time to his cousin, "and the Russian merry-making especially, with its folk dancers, its dancing and its drinking."

As for love, what an exquisite thing was a young girl,

with her fresh charm, laughing eyes and soft apple-blossom complexion! He had an artist's eye for beauty. And oh, the interest of living faces! The magic of conversation! Life was an enchanting pageant which held him in thrall, and although at the moment he was still a spectator, soon he would begin to live. Terrible and imperative was the will to live, inherited from elemental dust through countless generations. In the meantime, one must work incessantly, for time was so precious that not a moment was to be lost. He was, of course, often lonely, for as he walked home on summer evenings he saw, through the windows of houses, families gathered round the samovar for tea, and his heart ached unbearably as he watched their happy faces. At the Festival of Easter, too, he was particularly desolate, for Easter in Russia is the great event of the year. All families drew together at Easter. How poignantly he remembered other Easters, before poverty and disgrace had shattered the home and split the family.

The festivities would begin with Butter Week, a week of feasting and rejoicing, in preparation for the long fast (of seven weeks) ahead. During this week it was the custom to drive out in one's carriage, however fine or humble, in procession round the gaily decked booths, which were set out for the festivities. The prancing horses were brightly dressed, the bells and harness jingled, and the occupants of the carriages smiled and bowed to each other as they paraded. All wore their best clothes, and peasants in bright kerchiefs laughed and chattered on the sidewalks.

Then as the long fast drew to a close, expectation was excited to the uttermost, and when Easter Eve arrived people walked in hundreds from one church to another. Towards midnight, however, the churches gradually filled, and after a solemn Mass, and when the clock struck twelve, the fast was banished as if by magic. The golden doors of the Ikonstases were opened, and the chorus "Christ is risen! Christ is risen from the dead!" burst upon the ear. At the same moment every chandelier and wax taper was lighted, and the main body of the priests incessantly repeated the

B

strain "Christ is risen!" This was echoed on all sides, and people embraced each other, shook hands and kissed, saying at the same time "Christ is risen!" "He is risen, indeed" the other would reply. The priests then, in full pontificals, would come forward with censers, and as they paused before the image of each saint, would make their obeisance and repeat "Christ is risen!" The bells of the city would then strike up together, the streets and buildings were illuminated, guns were fired, and rockets would ascend from the barracks. After this, the congregation would walk in procession with tapers round the church, with the priests at their head, and between two and three a.m. the food was consecrated, people returned to their homes, and there was no end to the bowing and kissing and congratulations; in palace and cottage the Easter breakfast was a sumptuous feast.

It was Easter, too, which brought sad thoughts to Anton of his mother; she was one of those rare women who radiate happiness, but he realised that the loss of her home in Taganrog had almost crushed her, and her letters were heart-breaking. She was, however, convinced that life would be happier when Anton could come to Moscow, and she constantly implored him to join the family. Yet he was determined to finish his schooling and pass his examinations first. He therefore begged his cousin in Moscow to keep in touch with the family. "Please go on comforting my mother, who is both spiritually and physically broken," he wrote. Indeed, his parents were constantly in his thoughts. "If I should climb high it is the work of their hands," he said. "They are glorious people and their love of their children alone places them above all praise."

"If I should climb high!" Surely that phrase indicates that Anton had some inkling of what the future held! "If only I pass my matriculation exams I'll come flying on wings to Moscow," he wrote to his cousin, and he added, with youthful confidence, "When I get rich (and that I am going to become rich is as true as twice two is four) I shall feed you on cakes and honey and treat you to the best wine, for the fraternal devotion with which you respond to our respect and devotion."

Moscow! Moscow! That was the city of all his hopes and dreams, and every glittering cross on its hundreds of churches shone like a welcoming beacon to the lonely ambitious boy. For literature was his god, and although only sixteen he was deep in Shakespeare, Turgenev, Goncharov and Cervantes. The works of Tolstoy were also running through him like a stream of fire. Indeed, what a feast he had to choose from, for these magnificent writers could not be matched in all Europe, and he was determined to become an author. Medicine, too, interested him deeply, but as the profession of author was obviously precarious, he intended to qualify as a doctor and then to write in his spare time. That was his plan. The knowledge, too, that he could no longer rely upon the guidance of his parents hastened his development, and it was often he who gave advice to them, for already they had great faith in his judgment and intelligence. Sometimes they were in despair about the future, but Anton refused to be discouraged; he was determined that they should continue to hold up their heads. He was able, also, at times to assist them financially, though only at the cost of great personal sacrifice.

A proof of this dignified and courageous attitude is shewn by one of his letters to his younger brother Michael, at about this time. Michael had written to Anton and had apparently signed himself "Your worthless and insignificant brother"—a piece of self-depreciation to which Anton could not possibly subscribe.

"Why do you style yourself 'Your worthless and insignificant brother'?" asked Anton. "Not all Michaels, my dear fellow, must be alike. You recognise your in-significance? . . . Recognise it before God, certainly, and in the presence of beauty, intelligence and nature, but not before men. Amongst men you must be conscious of your dignity. Why, you are not a rascal. You are an honest man, aren't you? Well, respect yourself as an honest man and realise that an honest man is not something worthless.

Don't confound being humble with recognising one's worthlessness . . ."

In the meantime, Anton struggled on with his tutoring and his studies.   For three long years he was alone in Taganrog, but at the end of that time he was a mature man; his boyhood was left behind, and every member of his family believed that he alone would solve their problems, so great was their faith in him.

Chapter 2

The Undergraduate

WHEN Anton matriculated at the Taganrog High School at the age of nineteen he was in no doubt as to the path he was to choose. He believed that he could support himself by writing for the popular press, and at the same time he intended to study medicine. Doctors in Russia were very scarce and were badly needed, especially in country districts. He had obtained a scholarship of 25 roubles a month from the Taganrog Town Council. He had also arranged for two school friends, who were studying medicine in Moscow, to live with his family as boarders.

Anton joined his family in Moscow in the August following his matriculation, and when he arrived, the streets were hot and stifling. Nevertheless he was greatly impressed by this splendid city. The fine façades of its seven hundred monasteries, churches and cathedrals were decorated by gigantic saints, haloed in gold, while every dome and tower was surmounted by a glittering cross or spire. Monks and popes paraded the streets, crowds followed the religious processions, and the splendour and variety of the uniforms worn in the streets was astonishing. Civil and military officers, the teachers in the public schools, the professors of the Universities, the pupils in the gymnasium schools, were all uniformed, striped, dotted and garnished like butterflies. The army officers were particularly fine, and dressed as for a parade, with gleaming epaulettes, plumes and many stars.

The shops were extremely gay and colourful; the flower-markets, too, were lovely, and the white-walled houses, with their red and green roofs, seemed to nestle in a sea of verdure. But Moscow was perhaps most enchanting at night, when the dark streets were softly illuminated, and in the chemists' shops—of which there were many—the large round bottles filled with blue, yellow or red liquid were lighted; these could be seen at a great distance down the streets and produced the effect of chinese lanterns.

In spite of the climate it was the custom in Moscow for meals to be taken in the open air, and many delicious foods were sold in the streets. There were the women who sold new milk; they wore bright kerchiefs round their heads, scarlet sarafans over their clothes, long earrings, green shoes with red binding; and their hair hung down in one long tress with a bow of yellow ribbon. They balanced their tin milkcans and their round earthen cream jugs on a skilfully contrived yoke, upon one shoulder only, and their charming soft voices were delightful to listen to.

There was the flower-seller, too, with his pots on a board on his head, and the bird-seller, with his cages hung about him from head to foot. The men who sold fruit drinks and kvas set up their tables at the corners of the streets, and from these tables people were constantly going to carry refreshments to the markets and public places.

It was a most picturesque and interesting city. Yet was this only on the surface? It was obvious that poverty and misery existed, here as elsewhere. Indeed, at the doors of the churches and monasteries the beggars crouched in their rags. "Give alms, for Christ's sake!" they pleaded, as they turned up their mournful eyes to the passers-by.

Such was Moscow in summer, but in winter it was transformed. In October the snow began to fall, day after day, incessantly, and soon roofs, pavements and trees were covered by a thick white blanket. On a fine day hoar frost sparkled on the trees, and the sky was clear, cloudless and ethereally blue. From houses and churches, all of which were heated, thick columns of vapour arose, which reflected a myriad colours. It was like fairyland. Carts were now replaced by sleighs, and along the smooth frozen pavements they glided as agreeably and noiselessly as the gondolas along the canals of Venice.

The Russian sleigh, as the result of long experience and native ingenuity, was one of the lightest sleighs in the world, and one could hire an elegant equipage in the street. The rugs were lined with fur, and the driver, with his superb beard and kaftan, was most courteous, smiling and bowing continually. He would address his horse as "My pigeon", "my brother", "daddy", "my friend", "sweetheart", etc., and the horse himself, gay with bright harness and bells, seemed to bow his neck in acknowledgment of these endearments. The rich had their own fine sleighs, drawn by two or four splendid horses; the bells jingled melodiously, the handsome women in their fur coats and caps nodded and smiled as they greeted their friends in passing sleighs, and almost every pretty face had a look of rosy health caused by the tingling air.

Yet when the cold became really intense in Moscow it was a different story. The police began to be alert, and officers went the rounds day and night to keep the sentries awake; they would severely punish on the spot any man caught napping, as to sleep in such weather was the most certain way of dying. Faces were now muffled in furs, and the fear of losing eyes, ears or nose through the frost was a very real one. When the cold reached twenty-five degrees below zero the theatres were closed, and no child was allowed to venture out.

But the moment the thermometer rose a little, the tea-men began to parade the streets. With thick cloths wrapped round the tea-machine they cried to the passers-by "It boils! It boils!" They had cups and glasses ready, and lemons and hot cakes. Men with sledges of gingerbread, bon-bons and dainties also paraded the streets. Rosy-faced, shaggy-haired and bearded, and wearing thick gloves, bast shoes and sheepskins, they ran about crying "Hot! Hot!" They were the merriest, the most polite, and the best-tempered men in the world.

The arrival of Anton in Moscow was a great event to his family, and he found them living in a half-basement house in the Drachkovka quarter of the city. His father and the two eldest boys had found employment away from home, so Anton became the head of the household, a position he assumed quite naturally. "Anton", wrote Michael, "has taken the place of father, and father's personality has faded into the background." In appearance Anton was tall and broad-shouldered, and on his clear-cut face there was the unmistakable stamp of the intellectual, yet there was a country air about him, which both men and women found attractive. His eyes were blue, with a direct gaze, and he spoke simply and without affectation, yet he was an animated and admirable conversationalist, eager, interested and enthusiastic. He was quick to praise whatever and whoever pleased him, a trait which was one of his most engaging characteristics. Indeed, men meeting him for the first time said almost spontaneously "What a delightful fellow!"

Anton had decided to begin his medical studies at Moscow University almost immediately, but that heavy, grimy edifice was painfully unimpressive, for the gloomy corridors, depressing staircases and badly-lit rooms seemed to indicate a sad lack of progressive thought; the very coat-stands and benches wore an air of desolation. At the ugly, battered gates, too, lolled a bored caretaker in an old sheepskin coat, who, armed with a broom, gazed around at the dirty heaps of snow with a disconsolate and mournful air. Was he, one wondered, typical of what went on within? And would one, in a few years' time, be reduced to the same hopeless condition? It was a sobering thought.

Anton soon realised that his family were depending on him mainly for guidance, maintenance and support, as his father was obviously quite unable to bear the burden. He acknowledged the claim cheerfully, lovingly and almost unconsciously. It was not his nature to murmur over what was inevitable, or to plume himself on doing what was right. He was quite prepared to take responsibility without fear, to venture where others shrank, to decide where others wavered. As for literature, it would have to wait. But of this he was determined:—one day he would devote himself to serious writing, and only the very highest standard would satisfy him. The literature of the past had had an immense influence on Russia; it had taken in its stride all the most vital and profound problems of that vast country, and by the grace of God Anton intended to follow this tradition. Life seemed to him, in fact, at that time, "enchanting, marvellous and full of lofty meaning". The feeling of youth, breadth, vigour, and the knowledge that life held such splendid opportunities, almost took his breath away. He was young, healthy, ambitious, and the world was before him; it was his to conquer.

Chapter 3

Tchehov the humorist

M OSCOW University had for many years been the chief centre of the new intelligentsia in Russia. Its members were recruited partly from the educated nobility and partly from the sons of professional men, priests, doctors, etc. But the discipline was said to be lax, the standard of morals low, and the students were addicted to forming political clubs. It must be remembered, however, that the University was purely a Government institution, and its professors were really officials; they were paid simply to read the lectures, and therefore few of them took any interest in the moral and spiritual development of the students. The young Russian, burning with enthusiasm and ideas, loves discussions, but he had no opportunity to expound his views, as there were no debating societies or clubs of that kind; the students, in fact, had no outlet for their grievances, and any criticism could only be voiced in secret. In those days, also, there were no organised games or athletics, so the students were deprived of any outlet for superfluous energy and high spirits. It is not surprising, therefore, that the undergraduates were apt to brood on their own misfortunes and became discontented and "against the Government".

Many of the undergraduates were poor, and to earn the fees, which fortunately were very low, they were obliged to work in their spare time and in the vacations. Some of them gave lessons, others sang in the theatre choruses or played in orchestras, some even became ticket collectors on the railway. Tchehov began immediately to write for magazines and newspapers; (His brother, Alexander, had done the same). But it is obvious that he had little time to spare, as his medical work made heavy demands upon his time; there were constant lectures, post-mortems, etc. It was necessary, therefore, to write in the early hours of the morning and late at night. But success with his writing did not come at first, for many of his stories were rejected, not for any fault, but because his name was unknown, and editors are notoriously shy of accepting such work.

Tchehov's first published story appeared in a magazine called *The Dragon Fly*, and other short, humorous stories followed in quick succession. But he never for one moment intended that this work should be a serious contribution to literature; humorous work, on the whole, was easy to sell, and he wrote solely for the purpose of earning a living. To live, and to keep out of debt; these were the urgent problems, and they could only be solved by working incessantly, night and day.

His contacts with editors also brought opportunities for reporting and interviewing, work which he accepted gratefully. Yet how difficult his task was, for he was obliged to write (as he confessed to one of his editor friends) "under the most hideous circumstances! Before me is my non-literary work mercilessly whipping my conscience; in the next room howls the child of a relation who has come to stay with us; in the other room my father is reading aloud to mother 'The Flaming Angel'; someone has wound up the music box . . . my bed is occupied by a visitor, who comes up to me now and then and starts a talk on medicine. . . . . I long to run away to the country, but it is one o'clock in the morning."

Frequently, also, he was not paid for his work, as the magazine proprietors were generally short of money. And occasionally he was paid in kind; he might be asked to order a new pair of trousers from a tailor, or to take theatre tickets in lieu of payment. He could not afford to quarrel with editors. There were temptations, however, which he firmly resisted; his income might have been considerably increased if he had agreed to write for certain papers the sort of stories and articles they demanded. "It is better to

treat loathsome diseases than to take money for vile stories . . .
Let us wait and see, and meanwhile let us go in shabby
coats," he said.

Here was the idealist, inflexible and firm of purpose.
He considered that Literature was a sacred art with a far-
reaching influence, and not to be dragged in the dust. He
was willing to be humorous—indeed, that was his usual
vein—but editors must go elsewhere if they wished to
appeal to the lower side of human nature.

Yet it was at this time that a more serious note in
Tchehov's work began gradually to assert itself. Almost
against his will, he found himself turning from humour to
realism.

By the Spring of 1883 Tchehov was working in-
creasingly hard, yet the family could barely pay for the
necessities of life. "The hundred roubles I make a month
sink into the belly, and there's no chance to change my
shabby indecent jacket into something less ancient. I am
paying on all sides and there remains nihil to me" he
confessed to his brother. Ah, how he longed for leisure in
which to think and to work, calmly and without anxiety!
"I am a newspaper man because I write much" he confessed, "but this is only temporary . . . I shall not die one."
Inevitably there would come a time when he would produce
something better than these trifles. For, indeed, he had no
lack of material. What could be more inspiring than his
work as a medical student? The tragedies which he witnessed
daily, in hospital alone, could produce material for many
books. In addition, he frequently attended the Law Courts,
and in those doubtful Seats of Justice (the law was very
corrupt) he was able to observe the most varied types of
individuals, from the rich Moscow merchants and the
successful lawyers, to the vagabonds and riff-raff of the gutter.

His scientific studies, too, were deeply interesting, and
he was completely captivated by this new branch of learning.
"I tell you there is nothing more seductive and gracious,
nothing so seizes and overwhelms the human soul, as the
beginning of a science" says Likharyoll (in the story "On

the Road".)   And surely it is Tchehov himself speaking!
"In the first five or six lectures you are exalted by the very
brightest hopes; you seem already the master of eternal
truth . . . Well, I gave myself to science passionately, as to
a woman loved.   I was its slave, and except it, would
recognise no other one.   Day and night, night and day,
without unbending my back, I studied . . . "

But Tchehov's experience in the Law Courts disgusted
him, for apparently few Russian lawyers had any idea of
justice, nor did they believe in the sanctity of the law.   The
Courts were crowded by Presidents, superior and inferior
Judges, Assessors, etc., yet justice was not to be obtained.

The Moscow household consisted at this time of
Anton's mother, sister and two brothers (Michael and
Nicolay), an undergraduate friend, a cousin, and the kind
but stupid "Auntie", who used a noisy sewing-machine
with great energy.   Anton's father came in each evening,
and another brother paid daily visits and spent the
holidays there.   Anton had no room in which to work
alone, and his stories had to be written in a babel of noise
and conversation.   It was a gay and affectionate family,
but they were all noisy, talkative, financially irresponsible
and egotistical.   The willing horse was taken for granted.
As for Nicolay, who was supposed to be studying at the
School of Painting, he had grown slovenly, lazy, was rarely
sober, and made no contribution to the household expenses.
He had practically given up painting and was living the
life of a tramp, having continually to be rescued from the
gutter and kept at home almost by force.   "Not a day
passes" (Tchehov confessed to a friend) "without some
unpleasantness.   Again and again I come across some vile
piece of news, so that I am afraid even of receiving letters."

The problem of Nicolay, in fact, was a serious one, as
he could not settle to work and failed to carry out his
commissions.   He had also avoided his military service,
which was compulsory, and was in trouble with the police
as a result. Anton had arranged an exhibition of his paintings
in a Moscow art shop, but it was a waste of time and effort.

At this time, too, Alexander, the eldest brother, who also drank heavily, wished to join the household, accompanied by his children and nurse. (He was not legally married, and this fact, apparently, troubled his conscience.) He had resigned his post as a Customs official and was carrying on a hand-to-mouth existence in Moscow. But Anton was obliged to point out that he could offer no further hospitality. Indeed, the strain of responsibility, long hours, and anxiety over his brothers was beginning to undermine his health. At the end of a long day he was completely exhausted. "I long for rest" he confessed, "but the summer is still far away."

Chapter 4

The budding genius

IN the meantime, a journalist's job was not an enviable one, as the press was heavily censored, and every newspaper was constantly in danger of being suppressed. Life in Russia, in fact, was full of frustrations, and beneath the surface the country was seething with unrest and revolutionary feeling. There was an urgent need for drastic reform in every direction, as all independent activity by educated people was sternly discouraged, free speech was impossible, and even the rights and powers of the Local Authorities were constantly being cut down by legislative enactments. The Universities, Academies and Technical Institutes were often arbitrarily closed, and Professors were deprived of their Chairs, or else their positions became so intolerable that they voluntarily resigned. Since the end of the Crimean war thousands of young men and women had taken part in the campaign of terror against the Government, and as a result, hundreds had been exiled, either to Siberia, or to the extreme north of European Russia—a cruel punishment which was frequently imposed merely for attending meetings which in England or America would have been perfectly legal.

In addition, the various police regulations were most irritating. Whether entering or leaving the country, sending letters or parcels, buying or selling, walking, riding or driving, men and women were liable to police interference. It was necessary to visit the police when changing lodgings or when moving from one town to another. It was also necessary to obtain permission when hiring oneself as a servant, or even as a tutor to give lessons.

Since the emancipation of the serfs certain reforms, it

is true, had come into being, and much had been done to improve the condition of the lower classes. New Law Courts with public procedure had been instituted, trial by jury had been established, and conscription (which at one time had applied to certain classes only) had been extended to all classes. Jews had also been given access to the schools and to the liberal professions.

But these reforms were not really effective, for the agents of the Tsar never intended that they should succeed. The ruthless tyranny of the laws, too, effectually destroyed any benefits which might have accrued to the people. Finally, matters in Russia had come to a head. The Terrorists were weary of obeying the arbitrary caprices of the Tsars, and on March 13th, 1881, Alexander II was assassinated.

This act, which was universally condemned, did irreparable harm to the Socialist cause, for after the accession of Alexander III, a reaction against Socialism set in. The bureaucratic element in Russia was strengthened everywhere, and the police received extended powers to crush the revolutionary movement. The hard-won independence of the Law Courts and the Universities was abolished, and a series of counter-reforms was carried out, changes which actually tended to increase the legal and social gulf between the upper and lower classes.

These events were extremely depressing, as it was realised that no further reforms could be expected. And to Tchehov, in touch through journalism with contemporary thought, it seemed that the death knell of social progress had been sounded. He had never attempted to take an active part in the revolutionary movement, yet he deplored as much as any man the rottenness of the political fabric, the legal corruption, and the repression of all activity.

The lack of freedom, in fact, was at times terrifying. It haunted one like a spectre, it was constantly there, peering over one's shoulder, for the Government made no secret of the fact that spies and informers were everywhere. A few words dropped in casual conversation might result in a serious charge and a sentence of banishment. Then without a fair trial one might find oneself chained to a truck in Siberia, or groping in fetters through the narrow shafts of a mine. It was not a pleasant prospect.

It seemed to Tchehov, in fact, that for the masses of people life had inevitably lost its savour; frustration had done its deadly work and left behind a sense of bitter inertia. Why light a candle to shine in a naughty world when it would never be allowed to burn? Why dream of schemes for the betterment of man if they were to be strangled at birth? And if life, as a result, was no longer rooted in any deeper values, was it not bound to grow chaotic and ugly? Was not everything refined doomed beforehand? Would not every man seek merely to gratify his own desires and care nothing for his neighbour?

In the small towns, for instance, Tchehov was appalled by the stagnation of life, and the stupidity and mediocrity of those he met, even the so-called intelligentsia. So many people were unhappy and discontented; they whined and complained continually, yet they made no effort to get out of the dreary rut. They had lost heart, and the disease of apathy had spread; one saw evidence of it everywhere. But nothing could be done; it was like beating one's head against the bars of a prison.

Was this the reason why Tchehov's stories gradually became more serious in character? He was a high-minded youth—not an isolated artist—and inevitably influenced by his surroundings. He could, in fact, only write as nature dictated.

And now, too, he read and re-read the great Russian authors whose works he had always found so inspiring. There was Goncharov, whose theme of the "superfluous" man (the failure) was symbolic of so many Russians. There was also Uspensky, a writer of immense creative power, who had written brilliantly of the peasants and their problems. And there was, of course, that mighty genius (but irrational pagan) Tolstoy, whose insight into the human soul was as fine as anything in world literature.

C

His was a magic art which utterly defied definition. His joy in life and his full-blooded vitality had infected everything he touched, and he painted on such a vast canvas that one could only gasp and admire. As for Turgenev, who had done so much for the emancipation of the serfs, what a poetic genius was his! How tenderly, profoundly and delicately he had written of the peasants! How charmingly, and with what consummate art he had described rural life in Russia!

This literature had been produced in spite of the long years of terrorism and repression. And it had had its immense influence. The emancipation of the serfs had been achieved, and the intelligentsia had triumphed; in spite of the rigid censorship they had succeeded in presenting their views to an ever-growing audience. Why should any writer, therefore, be discouraged? For it was clear that what could not be achieved by political agitation could be achieved by the power of the pen. Indeed, Tchehov's head was buzzing with ideas for stories. They crowded into his brain with an insistence that would not be silenced. It was not restlessness, but the imperative voice of genius demanding to be heard.

In the meantime, mingling with these serious thoughts was that impish streak of humour—a saving grace. Nothing could quench it. Surely it was because life without humour would have been too horribly grim! At any rate, the young undergraduate could not resist the temptation to make a little humorous capital out of the political situation. One day, therefore, as he was riding in a cab through Moscow carrying a large parcel containing a pumpkin filled with pickles, he stopped the cab and solemnly handed the package to a policeman. "Take this" he said gravely. "It's a BOMB." And without another word he leapt into his cab and drove away.

The year in which Tchehov was working for his final examinations was a particularly difficult one, yet in order to fulfil his obligations he was obliged to maintain his literary output. Night after night he sat up writing; he

could not afford a moment's relaxation. His unflagging
energy, however, was equal to the task, and in May he
passed his "finals" and obtained his medical degree. But
the efforts of the past five years had completely exhausted
him, and a holiday of some sort was essential. For the
vacation, therefore, the family arranged to go to Voskressensk, where Ivan was working as a tutor.

The party was an extremely happy one, and they
spent their time in simple country pursuits—croquet, lawn
tennis, picking mushrooms, and fishing. Tchehov also
became friendly at this time with a very cultured and
musical family named Kiselyov, who owned a beautiful
estate, Babkino, near Voskressensk. Madame Kiselyov was
herself an author, and was the daughter of Begitchev, the
Director of the Moscow Imperial Theatre; she and her
family were intimate friends of Tchaikovsky, the composer,
and the Italian actor, Salvini.

There was at that time, also, a battery of soldiers
quartered at Voskressensk, and through Ivan (who was
tutor to the children of the Commander, Colonel Mayevsky)
Tchehov became acquainted with many of the officers, an
experience which proved extremely useful for his later
stories and for his play (written many years later) *The
Three Sisters*.

But this holiday was not spent in idleness, as every
morning he rose early and was already writing by seven
o'clock. His stories were now greatly in demand, and in
literary circles he was regarded as a talented young author
who was rapidly making a name for himself. He was
offered so much work, in fact, that he frequently recom-
mended other young writers—even his rivals—to editors.
And the stories he wrote now were of both town and
provincial life. He also wrote of the peasants, in whose
lives he was particularly interested. He liked to get into
conversation with them and to hear their views. He was
fascinated by their quaint and homely wisdom. "One
should always travel third-class" he said. "There you will
often hear most interesting things."

It is true that much had already been written about the peasants, and Turgenev and Grigorovitch, in particular, had set them up almost as mystical symbols of victimised innocence. Tchehov, however, had no illusions about the "Noble Savage", but what he did wish to emphasise was that the peasants were not merely economic cattle to be considered as a herd, but individuals, many of whom were much to be admired. Their courage and patience, for instance, were often remarkable. As for the many victims of life, those unfortunates who through ignorance or stupidity had come to grief, such men seemed to him to be particularly pitiable, for could they be blamed for their lack of intelligence? They could only reason with the faculties with which Nature had endowed them. The knowledge that peasants—both men and women—were still flogged, also filled him with indignation. The flogging took place in police stations, and a peasant had to pay 10 copecks for the privilege; that was for the rods and the labour.

On this holiday he found that his work was easier to arrange, and he wrote chiefly in the early hours of the morning, when all were asleep. But when the summer day drew to a close he and his friends would foregather on the terrace of the manor-house to talk. The gold and crimson sky would be reflected in the lake and in the whole air, which was still and pure, as it never was in Moscow. The geese would fly across the sky and the wildfowl would call softly. The conversation would be chiefly of literature, philosophy and the future of Russia, so hopelessly shrouded in gloom at that time. And while they talked, the moon would rise, and darkness would cover the countryside. This was the hour they loved, and when at last it was time to light the lamps and go indoors, a sigh would go up from the whole party. It was impossible that they could ever set the world to rights, but it was such a relief to air their views, to dream bright dreams for Russia, and for one evening fondly to believe that they might materialise.

During this holiday Tchehov acted as locum tenens to a young doctor in Zvenigorod, a small town near Voskressensk, and here most of his patients were peasants. The poor, illiterate, simple souls were not easy to treat, owing to their innumerable superstitions. They believed in witchcraft, for instance, and declared that stones could whistle and that fish could speak. Most of them, however, were truly pious, though their implicit faith in God made them foolishly resigned to their fate. "What God does is always for the best" they would say. The peasant women were particularly to be pitied, as they frequently died in childbirth, toiled from morning till night, became ill through working beyond their strength, grew old before their time and "died in filth and stench". How depressing, too, was the smell of the huts, the pot-house oaths, the un-washed children, the women's wailing, the continual talk of illness. It was difficult to be patient with the debauchery, the stupidity and the drunkenness. Sometimes whole villages were found intoxicated and in delirium tremens, and the peasants' weddings were merely drunken orgies, with raucous music, singing, chanting and dancing, which went on for hours.

The drunken peasant, however, was not as a rule quarrelsome; he became affectionate, maudlin, brimming over with universal philanthropy. He would kiss and embrace even his enemies, all bitterness forgotten. He was, in fact, a child that needed guiding. The excessive politeness of the average country peasant, too, was delightful; in saluting a friend he would take off his hat three times, shake him by the hand, call him brother, father, grand-father, and bow repeatedly. He would enquire with the kindest interest how he did, wish him the grace of God, the blessing of Heaven and the protection of all the saints. The peasants, in fact, were not bowed by the rod, nor debased before their worshipped tyrants; they had a natural dignity. Most of them were witty, too, never at a loss for an answer, and quick to make a humorous retort.

On his return to Moscow Tchehov wrote many stories of peasant life, and that autumn he was able to publish a small volume of stories called *Stories of Mel-*

pomena. It was his first book and contained some fine work, yet was hardly noticed by the press. Tchehov was also anxious at this time to start his work as a doctor, but apparently he had taxed his health severely. The long hours spent in writing, with very little rest, had taken their toll, and in December, while engaged on reporting a case in the High Court, he had a bad attack of haemorrhage from the lungs—a symptom of tuberculosis. His medical colleagues were seriously concerned and urged him to go abroad for his health; a long rest was imperative, either in some recognised health resort or in the Crimea. They did, in fact, make plans for him, and even offered to advance money, but he was obliged to point out that his family were almost entirely dependent on his earnings, and his financial position was still perilously insecure. To go abroad meant that he would have to resign his medical career and literature, a drastic step that was quite out of the question.

He remembered, incidentally, that he had been feeling unwell for some years, and that in Taganrog, at the age of seventeen, after bathing in icy water on a hot day, he had caught a serious chill and been extremely ill on the road; he had spent a night of agony in an inn. Possibly this present illness could be dated from that time.

Chapter 5

Recognition as a literary artist

TCHEHOV worked in Moscow all that winter as a
doctor, but his medical work proved disappointingly
unremunerative, as he was generous to a fault, and
his friends, apparently, expected to be treated and advised
without payment. Occasionally he was paid three or four
roubles a visit, but this sum barely covered his cab fares.
His literary work, however, was commanding better payment, and now he was no longer working for inferior
magazines and newspapers. Thanks to his friend Lakin he
had become a contributor to the *Petersburg Gazette*, in which
his stories *The Huntsman* and *A Horse-like name* appeared.
(*The Huntsman* was written in a bathing shed.)

But Lakin was anxious that this brilliant young
author should visit Petersburg, which was at that time the
centre of all literary activity. Tchehov, too, realised the
importance of such a visit, but the means were not forth-
coming. "Owing to the fact that we are a large family," he
wrote to Lakin, "I never have a ten-rouble note to spare,
and to go there, even if I did it in the most uncomfortable
and beggarly circumstances, would cost at least fifty roubles.
How am I to get the money?"

Lakin was nevertheless determined that his friend
should visit Petersburg. Tchehov was making a reputation
and it was essential for him to meet other authors and
editors. Therefore, a few months later (in December, 1885)
Lakin came to Moscow and took Tchehov back to Petersburg with him. They travelled by express, first-class, and
on arrival Tchehov was given "superb accommodation".
He was enchanted with the place; and, indeed, Petersburg
is at its best in winter. The cold was intense, and the ice

on the Neva was six feet thick, but in the squares and open places great bonfires were lighted at night for the benefit of the droshky drivers and the poor people.

Tchehov was received with almost overwhelming kindness and hospitality. He was "driven all over the city", presented with tickets for the theatres, and invited to meet all the most noted literary people. He was given a valet to wait on him, one who walked round on tiptoe, anticipating his every wish. (This he did not desire, but it amused him.) "I feel in the seventh heaven," he wrote to his brother. "Wise and decent men are so many that one simply has to pick. I make acquaintances every day."

But what proved most valuable to his future career was his introduction to A. S. Suvorin, the Editor and proprietor of the *Novoye Vremya*, the largest and most popular daily newspaper in Petersburg at that time. Suvorin was well known to Tchehov by reputation, as in addition to being a newspaper proprietor he was also a very talented writer and an extremely able critic. Although he came of peasant stock he was a man of the highest culture and intelligence.

At the great publisher's invitation Tchehov called at the offices of the *Novoye Vremya*, and he wore a new overcoat, new trousers and new boots. He was received by Suvorin very kindly, and after a long conversation it was arranged that the young author should become a regular contributor to the *Novoye Vremya*. But Suvorin was anxious that this promising young man should not waste his substance in riotous living, so before they parted he offered a few words of fatherly advice. "Take pains, young man," he said warningly. "I am satisfied with you, but you must go to church as often as you can, and *do not drink vodka*." Tchehov remembered, with horror, that he had just taken a glass of vodka with a friend. "Breathe!" commanded Suvorin, and Tchehov did so. But Suvorin made no comment and the two men parted as friends. Tchehov returned to Moscow in the very highest spirits, with all the depression and ill-health of the long winter forgotten. For were not his feet now firmly set on the ladder? He travelled back to Moscow first-class (as he had come) and he returned the richer by three hundred roubles.

His work in the *Novoye Vremya* now became a special feature, but he no longer used a pseudonym, and every story appeared under his own name. As for Suvorin, he was delighted with the new writer, and in February, 1886, he wrote to Tchehov and praised his work most generously, concluding with some valuable advice. "Thank you for the helpful advice," the young man wrote in reply. "I have been writing for six years, but you are the first person who has taken the trouble to advise and explain." He was, indeed, profoundly grateful. But the most enthusiastic tribute to Tchehov's work arrived a few weeks later when he received a letter from the celebrated writer, D. V. Grigorovitch. "I am past sixty-five," he wrote, "but I have still preserved so much love for literature, I follow its success with so much eagerness, I am so glad when I meet in it anything alive and gifted, that, as you see, I could not restrain myself, and I hold out to you both my hands . . . . You have a real talent, a talent that puts you far above the circle of writers of the new generation. . . . When you happen to be in Petersburg I hope to meet and embrace you, as I do now in your absence."

This charming letter made a great impression on Tchehov, for the burden of work and anxiety of the last six years had almost crushed his belief in his own talent. He had "knocked about from one newspaper office to another" and there had been little time for really serious work. All this Tchehov explained to Grigorovitch, and he confessed at the same time that he was a doctor by profession, so that it had been impossible to give to his literary work the care and thought he would have wished. "Your letter, my kind, fervently beloved bringer of good tidings, struck me like a flash of lightning," he wrote. "I was overwhelmed, and now I feel it has left a deep trace in my soul . . . I can find neither words nor deeds to thank you. . . . I am almost dazed. I have no power to judge whether I deserve this high reward. I can only repeat that it has overwhelmed me. If I have a gift which one ought to respect, I confess before the pure candour of your heart that hitherto I have not respected it. I felt that I had a gift but I had got into the habit of thinking that it was insignificant . . . Hitherto my attitude to my literary work has been frivolous, heedless, casual . . . I shall put an end to working against time but cannot do so yet . . . It is impossible to get out of the rut I have got into. I have nothing against going hungry, as I have done in the past, but it is not a question of myself . . . In the summer, when I have more time and fewer expenses, I will start on some serious work . . ."

Tchehov was at this time about to publish his second volume of stories, *Motley Tales*, but now he was ashamed of the book. It was, he felt, a "hotch potch", "a disorderly medley of stuff" which he had written as a student. It was not good enough. "Ah," he lamented to Grigorovitch, "had I known that I had readers and that you were watching me I would not have published this book. But I rest all my hopes on the future. I am only twenty-six. Perhaps I shall succeed in doing something, though time flies fast . . . ."

Motley Tales, in spite of the author's modest estimate of its worth, attracted a good deal of notice in the Press and many excellent reviews of the book were published in literary papers and monthlies.

But the praise of Grigorovitch and Suvorin encouraged Tchehov to give even more time to literature, and his health suffered as a result. In April, 1886, he was ill again and had another haemorrhage. However, he firmly refused to allow himself to be examined by doctors and went on as before with his work. There was neither the time nor the money for treatment. To go into hospital was out of the question, and a holiday was not yet due. He did however pay another visit to Petersburg on business, and on this occasion he stayed for two weeks and made the acquaintance of Grigorovitch.

Grigorovitch was an aristocrat in every sense of the word, but he was extremely emotional, and on meeting the young genius he was so overcome with pleasure and emotion that he collapsed, and Tchehov was obliged, there and then, to offer his services as a doctor. Tchehov was also able at this time to renew his acquaintance with Suvorin and the friends he had made on his previous visit. They were all very kind to him. It seemed, in fact, that every literary man in Petersburg was anxious to extend the hand of friendship to the young author; he had become the fashion. He had made a name.

Chapter 6

Fame

FAME, to a young author of twenty-six, is sometimes a little bewildering. Tchehov's work had been praised by eminent literary men, and there was no doubt of its excellence, yet as an artist always feverishly seeking for perfection, he was still dissatisfied with his achievements. He did not believe that his work had, as yet, any real or permanent value. Indeed, he declared that such success as he had achieved was due merely to a stroke of luck. "I feel ashamed", he confessed, "of the public which runs after lap-dogs because it fails to notice elephants, and I am deeply convinced that not a soul will know me when I begin to work in earnest."

Tchehov had, of course, been working in earnest for some time, for this mastery of his craft had not descended on him like a gift from God; it was the result of six years of strenuous endeavour and the most meticulous pains. But now here were the critics, comparing him with all the literary giants. It was said that his realism was almost equal to Gogol's, that the delicate lyricism of his stories had never been surpassed even by Turgenev, and that Goncharov himself might have envied his handling of "the superfluous man". But most of all was he praised for his warm, human sympathy. For his age, his work was astonishingly mature.

This was all very flattering, but fame had its drawbacks. How irritating and embarrassing, for instance, was the publicity that accompanied his success! He was continually bombarded by letters, even from strangers, asking for help and criticism; he was pointed out to people in the streets, and even his medical colleagues insisted on discussing literature with him on every possible occasion. His friends imagined, also, that he was making a fortune, for they constantly borrowed money without attempting to repay; they also took his books and wasted his time. "I am gradually turning into a dried dragonfly", he wrote to Madame Kiselyov, "and money is as scarce as cats' tears." He felt, indeed, "like a bone that has been thrown to the dogs". Domestic problems were also extremely harassing, as he was now apparently expected to shoulder all the responsibilities of the younger children's education. But his brother Nicolay was the greatest source of anxiety. Occasionally he roused himself, but he was really "idling his life away" and his work had become "vulgar and catchpenny". "There can't be two opinions about Nicolay being in the wrong," wrote Anton to his brother Alexander . . . "A greater muddler than our fool of a brother would be hard to find, and worst of all he is incorrigible . . . there is a good vigorous Russian talent going to the dogs . . . and going to the dogs for nothing. Another year or two and the artist will have sung his swan song . . ."

The family were seriously concerned about Nicolay's work and future, and finally it was decided to rouse the "misunderstood" brother, whose self-pity had become almost a vice. So Anton sat down and wrote a magnificent letter. It was not intended for posterity, but it surely deserves that honour:—

"I assure you", wrote Anton to Nicolay, "that as a brother and a friend I do understand you, and with all my soul I sympathise with you. I know all your good qualities as I know my five fingers; I value them and regard them with the deepest respect . . . In my opinion you are good-natured to the point of softness, you are magnanimous, not egotistical; you would share your last farthing; you are sincere; you are free from envy and hatred . . . you are trustful . . . you are gifted from above with that which others have not got; you have talent . . . But you have one failing . . . that is your utter lack of culture . . . You see, life has its conditions. In order to feel comfortable among educated people, to be at home and happy with them, one must be cultured to a certain extent. Talent has brought you into such a circle, you belong to it, but . . . you are drawn away from it, and you vaccilate between cultured people and the lodgers *vis-à-vis*.

Cultured people must, in my opinion, satisfy the following conditions:—

1. They respect human personality, and therefore they are always kind, gentle, polite and ready to give in to others. They do not make a row because of a hammer or a lost piece of indiarubber; if they live with anyone they do not regard it as a favour, and going away they do not say 'Nobody can live with you'. They forgive noise and cold and dried-up meat and witticisms and the presence of strangers in their home.

2. They have sympathy not for beggars and cats alone. Their heart aches for what the eye does not see . . . They sit up at night in order to help P . . . to pay for brothers at the University, and to buy clothes for their mother.

3. They respect the property of others and therefore pay their debts.

4. They are sincere, and dread lying like fire. They don't lie even in small things; a lie is insulting to the listener and puts him in a lower position in the eyes of the speaker. They do not pose, they behave in the street as they do at home, they do not show off before their humbler comrades. They are not given to babbling and forcing their uninvited confidences on others. Out of respect for other people's ears they more often keep silent than talk.

5. They do not disparage themselves to arouse compassion. They do not play on the strings of other people's hearts so that they may sigh and make much of them. They do not say 'I am misunderstood' or 'I have become second-rate'; because all this is striving after cheap effect, is vulgar, stale, false . . .

6. They have no shallow vanity. They do not care for such false diamonds as knowing celebrities, shaking hands with the drunken P . . ., being renowned in the taverns.

If they do a pennyworth they do not strut about as if they
had done a hundred roubles' worth and do not brag of
having the entry where others are not admitted . . . The
truly talented always keep in obscurity among the crowd,
as far as possible from advertisement . . .

7. If they have a talent, they respect it. They
sacrifice to it rest, women, wine, vanity . . . They are
proud of their talent . . . Besides, they are fastidious.

8. They develop the aesthetic feeling in themselves. . .
They seek as far as possible to restrain and ennoble the
sexual instinct . . . They want, especially if they are artists,
freshness, elegance, humanity, the capacity for motherhood.
. . . They do not swill vodka at all hours of the day and
night . . . They drink only when they are free, on occasion . . .

This is what cultured people are like. In order to be
cultured and not to stand below the level of your surroundings, it is not enough to have read *The Pickwick Papers*
and learnt a monologue from *Faust* . . . What is needed is
constant work, day and night, constant reading, study,
will . . . Every hour is precious for it . . . Come to us,
smash the vodka bottle, lie down and read . . . You must
drop your vanity, you are not a child . . . You will soon
be thirty . . . It is time."

But of what use were words to a man of Nicolay's
type? He had sunk too low. His health, too, was rapidly
deteriorating, as his foolish excesses were at last taking their
toll; as a doctor Tchehov saw the signs only too clearly.
He had made every effort to save him from his own folly,
but without success, and when at night, as Tchehov sat
writing in his room, the drunken footsteps went stumbling
past his door, he could only sigh for the wasted years, the
talent thrown away, the life that had become a burden.
For, indeed, Nicolay was desperately unhappy; one could
hear him moaning and muttering in his sleep. What would
become of him?

Chapter 7

Journey to the Holy Mountains

THE year of 1887 began happily for Tchehov, as on New Year's Day all the papers to which he contributed presented him with a compliment, and in the *Russkoye Bogatstvo*, for which Tolstoy wrote, there appeared a long article by Obolensky in which Tchehov's work was very highly praised. His superb story *Mire* also appeared at this time, and its principal character, the vivacious and interesting Jewess, was much discussed. But Tchehov was rather severely taken to task for the tone of this story by his friend, Madame Kiselyov. She apparently disapproved of stories on such subjects. But Tchehov stood his ground firmly. He was not in the least ashamed of the story.

"Everything in this world is relative and approximate" he declared. "There are people who can be demoralised even by children's books, and who read with particular pleasure the piquant passages in the Psalms and in Solomon's Proverbs, while there are others who only become the purer from closer knowledge of the filthy side of life. Political and social writers, lawyers and doctors who are initiated into all the mysteries of human sinfulness are not reputed to be immoral . . . To think that the duty of literature is to unearth the pearl from the refuse heap means to reject literature itself . . . The vocation of literature is to be absolutely true and honest . . . To a chemist nothing on earth is unclean. A writer must be as objective as a chemist. . . . . Writers are the children of their age and therefore like everybody else must submit to the external conditions of the community. Thus, they must be perfectly decent . . . But no thinking will discover a better police for literature than the critics and the author's own conscience. People have been trying to discover such a police since the creation of the world, but they have found nothing better."

Tchehov was now a great favourite with the public, and he was overwhelmed with invitations and orders. His works were read aloud at literary gatherings and the devotees of art and literature all sought to make his acquaintance. His medical practice, too, was increasing, but often it involved great strain and tired him almost to the point of exhaustion. "I have not a day of peace", he wrote to his uncle, "and I feel as though I were on thorns every moment." On his mother's birthday he was almost dropping with fatigue, and it was evident that a change of air and scene was essential, so eventually he was persuaded to go to Taganrog to visit his uncle. The idea of revisiting the home of his childhood suddenly appealed to him. Besides, he felt the urge to travel, to see more of Russia, and after Taganrog he could wander at will. In his youth the steppe had always fascinated him; he wished to write about it, to re-create those vivid colourful pictures which had stamped themselves upon his mind as a boy. He also planned to visit the Monastery in the Holy Mountains, and to talk with the monks there. That strange, austere life, dedicated to God, could surely be explained, and he was drawn by some strong attraction to these people, though not, it is true, from any religious point of view. It was merely that their admirable lives seemed to him worthy of study.

He left Moscow by train, and as the familiar landmarks came into view he experienced almost the same wonder and delight as when he had passed them as a boy. He saw his old friends, the ravens, flying over the steppe, and everything went past him "like a dream"—the shining rivers, white huts, oxen, daughters of landowners and farmers, the water-towers, the ancient barrows, the stone figures placed there long ages ago, the waggons in long trains, piled high with wool, and the horses lurching and staggering. The steppe was rich and luxuriant, with the loveliest wild flowers of every colour, and even from the train one could smell the scents. There were strange blue

D

birds along the roadside, hawks hovered in the sky, and the windmills in the distance looked like tiny men waving their arms.

But Taganrog, after the glories of Petersburg and Moscow, seemed but a poor place. The houses were shabby, the roofs needed painting, the shutters were closed. Threading his way through the new bazaar he realised how "dirty, drab, lazy and illiterate" the town was; there wasn't a single grammatical signboard, the plaster was peeling from the houses, the streets were deserted. Here, too, were the squares where men had often been flogged. Indeed, the pettiness of life in a provincial town struck him with horror. How tedious it all was! What boredom! Was this the place he had once thought so fine? It had changed; it was dreary beyond description.

Nevertheless he could not resist the temptation to go and visit his old home, but that too looked empty and deserted; it was horribly depressing. "How could we have lived in it?" he asked himself. The Cathedral, however, was just as beautiful, and its calm and holy atmosphere brought back tender memories of his youth. Here he had sung as a child. Before these candles and these images he had bowed his infantile head. It seemed so long ago. Ah, how time was passing!

In the meantime the weather had deteriorated, so he continued his journey and went on to Ragozina Balka, where he had arranged to stay with friends. Again he had to travel across the steppe, and incidentally spend the night in a second-class railway carriage in a siding. But what an unforgettable night that was, for there was a brilliant moon, and for some reason sleep would not come, so he walked out into the steppe. Here were "veritable marvels, the moon, the limitless steppe, the barrows, the wilderness, a deathly stillness . . . It seemed as though the world was dead." It was a scene which remained in his memory for years. For could one ever be saturated with beauty? It is true there was something of infinite sadness here too, which brought to the surface the heart's yearning and continual seeking, the hopeless quest of the artist. But that must be accepted; it was a part of life.

The house in which he stayed at Ragozina Balka was a small thatched one, and the conditions were extremely primitive. Apparently there were vipers under the bushes, and numbers of fierce watch-dogs barked continually and refused to allow anyone to pass, day or night, so Tchehov was obliged to go about under escort, "to avoid being torn to pieces". It was rather a hair-raising experience. However, the weather was fine, the grass was tall and in flower, one evening there was "a beautiful thunderstorm", and there were turkeys' eggs to eat!

From Ragozina Balka he went on to the Holy Mountains, and having to spend one night at Slavyansk he found pleasant lodgings and woke next day to a glorious morning; there was a scent of acacia and lilac, nightingales were singing, and the air was full of the ringing of bells. He drove out of the town "through little streets literally drowned in the green of cherry, apricot and apple trees", and the roads were filled with pilgrims. Walking and riding, they were now nearing the end of their journey.

And so at last he came to his destination, the Holy Mountains, where at the Monastery, picturesquely situated on the bank of the river Donetz, he was given hospitality for two nights. Some fifteen thousand pilgrims had assembled there to celebrate St. Nicholas Day, and the majority of them were old women, many of whom had come from long distances. They had come—as was the custom in the Middle Ages—for the fulfilment of a vow, or to pray for some sick child or husband. Many had come hoping to be cured of their infirmities. To those who needed medical advice and treatment Tchehov was delighted to be of service. The monks, too, sought his assistance, as doctors were scarce in that part of the country. He was treated as an honoured guest, and was much impressed by the kindness and hospitality shown by these simple, holy men. They fed the multitude of pilgrims with cabbage soup and meat, prayed and sang with them, and blessed them all. It was a moving experience.

Tchehov was quite touched with the small bedroom allotted to him; there was something charming about the scent of cypress, the simplicity and frugality, and the scrupulous cleanliness. As the monks passed down the corridors he noticed that almost every face wore an expression of courage and kindliness, and they spoke in warm, friendly tones. Here life could be as calm and unruffled as a summer's evening, and the outer world, with its stress and strain, thrust far away. Was there not something very beautiful about all this?

The nights at the monastery, however, were far from peaceful, and sleep was impossible, for the services were endless. At midnight the bells rang for Matins, at five for early Mass, at nine for late Mass, at three for the Song of Praise, at five for Vespers, at six for special prayers. And before every service a monk ran along the corridor ringing a bell and crying in an imploring voice, "Lord Jesus Christ, have mercy upon us! Please come to Matins."

This interesting holiday provided Tchehov with much useful material, and on his return to Moscow he wrote several stories based on his experiences. His impressions of the steppe, too, were recorded in a story of that name which appeared in the *Severny Vestnik* and created quite a sensation in Petersburg. This magazine was one of the best monthlies of that time, and Tchehov soon became a regular contributor. But what he did not know then, yet learnt later, was that police spies had followed his movements continually during his travels, one spy giving place to another. Indeed, he discovered that a spy had shared the same room with him in the monastery, under the plausible pretext that there was no room in the hostel.

All writers in Russia, in fact, were suspect at that time, and were continually watched and spied upon.

Chapter 8

"Ivanov"

AFTER the publication of his two new books, *In Twilight* and *Gloomy People*, Tchehov embarked on a new venture, the writing of a play. He had always wished to write for the theatre, but actually *Ivanov* was written at the invitation of E. A. Korsh, a theatrical manager in Moscow, whose theatre at that time produced light comedies and farces.

Ivanov was written at white heat, in about two weeks, and when it was finished it was shown to several people, all of whom were enthusiastic and prophesied success, but Tchehov himself was uncertain as to its merits. It was undoubtedly a very original play, and he had copied no one. But it was obvious that the *moods* of the characters were highly important. The whole action of the play, in fact, revolved round this "atmosphere".

Tchehov attended some of the rehearsals, but was quite bewildered by the behaviour of the actors. They quarrelled continually and, with two exceptions, appeared to have only the vaguest idea of their parts. "They acted through the prompter and by inner conviction." In Tchehov's opinion, too, most of the players were wrongly cast, and few of them seemed to understand the play. Indeed, as the rehearsals proceeded he regretted having written the piece, but to withdraw it at the last moment was impossible.

Ivanov was presented on the 19th November, 1887, to a full house—a select audience—and obviously there were great expectations. But the majority of the audience had come prepared to see a gay farce written in the manner of the author's humorous stories. They were not prepared for anything so serious as *Ivanov* proved to be.

Tchehov sat behind the scenes in a tiny box "like a prisoner's cell", and his family, trembling with apprehension, watched from a box on the pit-tier. The actors were very nervous, and continually crossed themselves. But from the moment the curtain rose Tchehov barely recognised a word of his own play, and one of the actors, on whom he had placed great hopes, did not speak "a single phrase correctly". Nevertheless, apparently the audience were satisfied, as the first act was applauded, and there were many calls.

In the second act it seemed to Tchehov that the actors were making a horrible fiasco of the whole thing; every word "cut him like a knife". The third act was a little better, as the players had lost their nervousness and were acting with more confidence. And now came Act 4, where in the second scene the curtain rose on a wedding party. There was a long supper table, with music and gaiety. But to the horror of the author the groomsmen played like clowns and turned the scene into a "merry-go-round and pothouse".

After this scene Kissielovsky entered, and a very beautiful passage was to follow, but he did not appear to know the part, and what should have been a most moving scene was changed into something "drawn-out and abominable". The audience were bewildered, and when at last the hero died (an ending which Tchehov disliked but which was insisted on by the actors) there was both tremendous applause and a good deal of hissing. The whole theatre, in fact, was in an uproar, and such excitement amongst the audience and on the stage had not been seen there for thirty-two years. Two men were ejected by the police, and one of the actors had an attack of palpitations. It was a wild evening.

The critics the following morning were very divided in their opinion of the play. One paper praised it, and another described it as "impudently cynical and immoral rubbish". But few people had really understood the piece. They had come to the theatre expecting to be amused, and

when they found that *Ivanov* was not a farce, they had felt
cheated and disappointed. Tchehov had made a reputation
as a humorist; they did not understand him in serious mood.

There is, however, little doubt that one of the chief
reasons why *Ivanov* caused so much controversy was that the
author's dramatic method was at that time quite new to
the theatre. Even the characters were unusual. Where, for
instance, was the traditional stage villain, the traditional
hero and the indispensable clown? No play, surely, could
be complete without these! But the characters in *Ivanov*
were far more complex. It was impossible for Tchehov to
create a set of theatrical puppets.

It has also been said of *Ivanov* that the dominant note
is one of hopelessness, that there appears to be no outlet
for the characters in their striving against fate—a criticism
which has some justification, for a sense of fatality certainly
runs through the whole piece. But this was very true of
Russia at that time. Life was hemmed about with arbitrary
laws and frustrations. "There is no law in Russia," said
Pushkin. "The law is nailed to a stake and that stake
wears a crown."

From the dramatic point of view, however, the theme
of *Ivanov* was probably too subtle. It was clear that the
conflict between the principal characters arose from the
fact that an enthusiastic and idealistic young man, frustrated
by an autocratic Government, had become discouraged and
melancholy. This type of failure, or "superfluous man", was
a product of the age, and in presenting *Ivanov* Tchehov was
saying, in effect, "Now I will show you what becomes of
the best brains, the most sensitive citizens, under the present
regime. There is no hope for Russia unless these men can
be encouraged instead of thwarted." He believed implicitly
in the individual.

But this theme could not be expected to appeal to a
theatre audience. Besides, the author had not attempted to
solve the problem, as he considered that to combine art
with a sermon was not the function of the artist. "It was
for the artist merely to select what was significant, to throw

light on the characters and to speak their language." Tchehov could not solve the problem of the frustrated individual; only a radical change in Russia's whole policy could do that. The most that could be expected of him was to draw the picture and point the moral. He had no particular faith in revolution, for to set the world on fire in order to build on the ashes was not his way. History showed that this created far more problems than it solved. As for the audience, their attitude appears to have been "Let us be gay, merry, without thought for the future, and if dramatic authors must make a hero of the "superfluous man" we will not listen; it is all too disturbing."

Tchehov, in fact, admitted that in writing the play he had endeavoured to say the last word on the traditional Russian hero's disillusionment. But he confessed to Suvorin that he ought to have waited. For such a theme maturity was essential; talent and good material were not enough. Also, "the feeling of personal freedom", which had only just begun to develop in himself, was essential. "Ah," sighed Tchehov, "what writers belonging to the upper class have received from nature for nothing, plebeians acquire at the cost of their youth."

Ivanov was performed a second time, with certain alterations, on the 23rd November, and the financial result, from both these performances, was satisfactory. For this he was grateful, for there were many calls on his purse, and financial problems were a constant anxiety.

When the excitement and discussion over the play had subsided, Tchehov once more resumed his literary and medical work, yet he confessed to Suvorin that he had as yet neither the energy nor the solitude to write as he would have wished. But what he did write at this time, being temporarily "bitten" with the theatre, was *The Proposal*, a clever and amusing farce. This was published in Suvorin's paper, *Novoye Vremya*, and became so popular that it was frequently played at Court by command of the Tzar.

So did the young author's reputation extend even into royal circles. As a humorist he was supreme, and although

as he gradually came to grips with life his stories became
more serious in tone, yet the merry twinkle in his eye
would not be dimmed. How he loved a good joke! As for
a comical and absurd situation, no one enjoyed it with
greater relish.

Chapter 9

The Pushkin prize

FOR the summer vacation of 1888 Tchehov rented a small lodge in the country belonging to an old estate at Soumy (in the Province of Harkov) which was owned by a Madame Lintvariov. The lodge was situated in a romantic spot on the banks of the river Psyol. There were old, neglected orchards and "sad, poetical manor-houses, nailed up and deserted". There was even a watermill, and the miller had a daughter, "who sat all day long at the window, as if waiting for something".

But perhaps the greatest attraction at Soumy was the fishing. It was Tchehov's favourite pastime, and on the green banks of the river he would sit for hours. He had become a rather silent person, but suddenly he would say thoughtfully, "London is a fine place". "But why London?" his companion would ask. "Because there", he would reply, "you can go out into the street and preach a new religion and nobody says a word to you." Ah, how he valued freedom, the lack of which in Russia was such a tragedy!

In Soumy there was all the musical and literary society he could desire, and the Lintvariovs at the big house were extremely kind. The family consisted of three daughters and two sons, and as cultured people who were interested in all the arts, they took a great fancy to Tchehov.

Plescheyev, the poet, also came to stay at the lodge, and although he was an old man and in feeble health the inhabitants of Soumy paid great homage to him as a celebrated author. Young girls in particular were very attracted to Plescheyev; they flattered him shamelessly, brought him bouquets, and drove him about to neighbouring estates. The old man used to compose his works aloud, and occasionally, when inspiration was at its height, his voice would rise to a shout. Tchehov, in real alarm, would rush into the room, but the old man would simply smile and go on with his work.

After Plescheyev's departure Suvorin arrived on a visit. He and Tchehov were now great friends and were both passionately fond of fishing. Sometimes they fished all day and all night, and discussed literature interminably. Indeed, it was impossible to be in Suvorin's company and keep silent; his views were so original and he had such a tremendous enthusiasm for life. Also, according to Tchehov, he had "superb taste" and had "developed his instincts to the dimensions of a great mind". Suvorin was a great lover and connoisseur of the theatre, he was the centre of the literary and artistic group in Petersburg, and he was a fine critic.

When fishing palled at Soumy it was amusing to drive out to neighbouring estates, with a four-in-hand, in a very ancient but comfortable carriage. They would visit some "romantic but crumbling and decrepit" mansion. The place had once been great and fertile but was now old and neglected. The house had sunk, the doors would not shut, young suckers of trees had grown through the cracks and windows, and birds had nested above the shutters. Everything was poetical and melancholy, but extremely beautiful. And the evenings, when the rosy sunset was reflected in the shining pools, were enchanting. "In fact", said Tchehov, "one might sell one's soul to the devil for the pleasure of looking at the warm evening sky."

There is no doubt that this holiday at Soumy inspired Tchehov to write his play *The Cherry Orchard*, the theme of which is the disintegration of a country estate and its eventual sale to a merchant. The owner, surrounded by her old servants, and one or two worthless "hangers-on", is heavily in debt, but failing to realise her position, makes no effort to avert the disaster—a truly Russian trait. This, indeed, is typical of what was happening at that time. The large estates, heavily mortgaged, were gradually

passing into the hands of the rich merchants. For the
owners, often deeply in debt, had lived far beyond their
means, invariably gambled recklessly, and were finally
obliged to sell. The emancipation had robbed them of
their serfs, and they could not adjust themselves to the new
order.

On Tchehov's return to Moscow in September,
Suvorin begged him to change his way of life. He urged
him to give up his medical work and devote himself entirely
to literature. It was surely impossible to follow two professions. But Tchehov could not agree. He was proud of
his medical work and it was an important part of his life.
It brought him into contact with many people whom
otherwise he would never have met. There were patients,
too, in whom he was deeply interested. These people
depended upon him for advice and treatment; he could not
fail them. It was pleasant, also, to feel that he had two
professions; when he was tired of one he could turn to the
other.

So he continued his work as a doctor. His vaudeville,
The Bear, was also written at this time, and was produced
at Korsh's theatre that season. This piece had a long run,
it was performed both in Petersburg and Moscow, and was
a financial success. But in October Tchehov's real triumph
came, as he was awarded the Pushkin prize for literature,
which amounted to 500 roubles. This tribute apparently
overwhelmed his family with happiness. Congratulations
from the public and the press also poured in, and Tchehov
was "fêted like a national hero". "They regale me with
food and drink like a General at a wedding," he said.

But though he continually joked about the prize, yet
he was genuinely moved by the knowledge that his contemporaries were anxious to recognise his work. He was
deeply touched because he felt that they were being extremely generous to him. He honestly believed that his
stories did not deserve the praise he received, nor would he
admit that his work had any permanent value. "All I have
yet written," he confessed, "and for which I have been

awarded the prize, will not survive even for ten years . . .
I have had a terrific run of luck . . . and I must hide myself
quickly under the table and sit there, quiet and meek, and
not raise my voice."

Now, too, he felt that at all costs he must justify the
award, and the praises lavished upon him. Therefore, he
began to write slowly and with much care, and he was
almost afraid to publish his work. He feared that readers
might soon tire of him. "And that fear", he explained, "has
a basis. I have been publishing for a long time . . . but
even yet I do not know in what is my strength and what
my weakness."

Tchehov's doubt as to the value of his own work was
increased also by the fact that in Russia at that time there
was almost a complete absence of good critics. Criticism
there was, of a kind, but most of it was worthless. Few, if
any, of these said critics had the courage to praise a new
writer, yet before an established reputation they bowed
their heads. In Tchehov's opinion they were all "lackeys
and cowards", afraid to back their own judgment. There
were others, of course, who did honestly seem to appreciate
his work, yet these same people invariably misinterpreted
and misunderstood his stories. So the question was forced
upon him:—For whom did he write? Was it for the masses,
who were uneducated, badly brought up and incapable of
discriminating between good and bad literature? No,
obviously their praise of his work was of little value. Yet
praise from literary societies and young women was equally
worthless, as it was clear that they did not understand his
work.

The announcement that Tchehov had been awarded
the Pushkin prize was made public on the 19th October,
1888, and the news was received in literary circles with
general approval. Nevertheless, in certain quarters there
was some envious comment. Many writers were, apparently
"as jealous as pigeons". So concerning his new honour
Tchehov made only one observation—"If I did not deserve
the Pushkin prize then any envy it arouses is false, and

only my equals and those who are better than myself can justly envy me or grumble."

Tchehov's new honour also produced a good deal of discussion as to what message this young writer had to give to the world, and Suvorin, always with one finger on the pulse of literary feeling, suggested to his friend that the time had come when his stories should indicate some solution of life's problems, or expound some philosophy. This suggestion, however, was not a new one to Tchehov; others had already hinted at something of the sort. But he had his answer ready:—He was not a prophet and he had no message. He was, in fact, impatient of generalities masquerading as progress. "It is time that writers," he said, "especially those who are artists, recognise that there is no making out anything in this world, as once Socrates realised, and Voltaire, too . . . The mob thinks it knows and understands everything, and the more stupid it is the wider it imagines its outlook to be. But if a writer whom the mob believes in has the courage to say that he does not understand anything of what he sees, that alone will be something gained in the realm of thought and a great step in advance."

It would, of course, have been easy for him, had he been less honest, to have propounded a philosophy of life, but he realised that human nature is far too complex to be made whole by one universal medicine, and he distrusted profoundly the sort of man who could say "Here is the truth and the only truth". Such men could always command an audience, for the yearning multitude loves a new philosophy. "How shall we live?" they cry. "You are a writer and a thinker. You can tell us." But was not the market-place always crowded with men who believe they have a special message of divine inspiration? And although such men may be passionately sincere, they are rarely first-class artists. Shakespeare had no message, or philosophy, even as a young man; that was evident from his work. He held up the mirror to life with a burning intensity of vision that could not lie, and he unfolded this vision with a magnificently detached impartiality.

It might be argued, of course, that it was the duty of every writer to hand on some message for humanity, since even a philosophy which has outlived its day has been of some service to mankind in assisting towards that culture in which Tchehov firmly believed. Yet his admirers felt that his work was making a very real contribution towards that culture, revealing as it did, with admirable impartiality, the causes of the spiritual ills of all classes of people. The Russian peasant, for instance, had been regarded for centuries as merely a poor ignorant beast, stupid and insensitive to suffering. Tchehov showed that the peasants were often more to be pitied than blamed, and that their insensitivity was a weapon with which they had fought out a long and dreary existence. Without education, or leisure, and devoid of any hope of improving their lot, is it surprising that many of them became sullen, morose, grasping, immoral and dishonest?

Tchehov's emotional penetration and breadth of insight had, in fact, achieved for the peasants' cause far more than any preaching could have done. He had painted their sorrows and tragedies with a vivid brush, and although in some circles he had been sharply criticised for endeavouring to champion their cause, he had his answer. When they asked, "Why write of failures?", and condemned his monk (*Easter Eve*) as a failure, he said "But how is he a failure? God grant us all a life like his. He believed in God . . . and he had the gift of composing poetry . . . To divide men into the successful and unsuccessful is to look at human nature from a narrow, preconceived point of view. Are you a success or not? Am I? Is Napoleon? Is your servant Vassily? What is the criterion? One must be a god to be able to tell successes from failures without making a mistake." How true this was! By his stories, in fact, Tchehov showed that tolerance and a deeper understanding of many failures might have turned them into useful and happy citizens. But men, he decided, when they failed to understand something, rarely searched for the cause in themselves, but blamed anything else within reach—other people, the Government, or the laws—hence the war with what they did not understand.

But of these controversial matters regarding his work he spoke only to the chosen few of his friends, as he loathed "serious discussions". Besides, he had decided quite early in his career that it was a breach of literary etiquette to reply to criticism. He insisted that authors should meet every criticism, however abusive or unjust, "with a silent bow". This was his wise and dignified policy. To excuse oneself, or defend one's work, could only lead to endless arguments.

Chapter 10

"The Wood Demon"

IT was at the end of the year 1888 that Suvorin decided to produce *Ivanov* again, and a good deal of correspondence passed between Tchehov and himself on the matter. But Tchehov felt that the play was an immature piece of work with which he had never been satisfied; he was not anxious to see it revived. On the other hand, from a financial point of view, the proposition was tempting. He still had many responsibilities; his mother and father were growing old, and his brother Michael had not yet finished his education at the University, where he was studying law, a profession which demanded a long and expensive training. Tchehov was generally able to keep free from debt, but there was never a penny of his income to spare.

They had now moved from their sordid surroundings and had taken a small, elegant little house. It was painted red, and owing to its rather severe architectural style it was known as "the chest of drawers". But there was a fine spiral staircase and some good rooms. There was a piano in the drawing-room, and in Tchehov's study his collection of books—many of which had been presented to him by Suvorin—made a modest but handsome library. The household was still a noisy one, yet at least for certain hours of the day he was able to work in peace. Marie was now teaching at a private school for girls, and also taking lessons in Art. As for the one-time grocer (who was now very proud of his famous son) he had apparently steadied his course a little, and his enthusiasm for music had given place to a passion for long sessions of prayer. Kneeling before the ikons he prayed interminably, and always aloud;

there was still, apparently, so much to pray for.

Life would have been very pleasant, in fact, for Tchehov at this time except for the lack of leisure, but in order to keep the wolf from the door incessant and un-remitting work was imperative. He was never free for a moment from the urgent and compelling thought that he must write; he was like a spider spinning a never-ending thread. Another gnawing anxiety, too—though he refused to allow himself to dwell on it—was the knowledge that his health was deteriorating. As a doctor he knew that he was suffering from a slow type of tuberculosis, and although he might, of course, live for many years, yet inevitably the day would come when he would no longer be able to work. There would probably come a time when his fine peasant constitution—which had stood so much—could no longer fight this dreadful disease. He was certain that he would never live to be an old man, and for all he knew, death might be just round the corner.

Work, therefore—while there was time—was im-perative, and he must do his utmost to increase his income, so that his family—for whom he had made himself res-ponsible—could be started in life, and his old parents securely settled with an income. That was his ambition. His mother and aunt, it is true, were continually planning, in the old Russian fashion, to marry him to a rich heiress. Was he not famous, handsome, admired and sought after? Did not women run after him shamelessly, send him their photographs, beg for interviews, and even propose to him? If he could marry a rich wife all their anxieties would be at an end, they said.

But Tchehov could not possibly agree; that was not his idea of marriage. He had, it is true, admired many women, and marriage—with the right woman—would have been delightful. But would this family, this dear Octopus, ever want to share him with a wife? They would never relinquish their hold, for this acceptance of him as their natural provider had existed too long; they took it for granted. He did not blame them, for he had himself accepted the burden; there had seemed to be no alternative. But when he did marry—and that day was probably far hence—he intended to give his whole heart to his wife. He had strong views about marriage, and they could not be changed at his time of life. As to this sordid but necessary question of finance, surely the theatre was the most paying proposition. A successful play could be written in less time than one of his long "short stories", and the financial reward was far greater. To write for the theatre again was, in fact, a great temptation, and he felt bound to consider Suvorin's plan to revive *Ivanov*.

On the other hand, Tchehov had to admit that he was somewhat afraid of the theatre, for the theatregoing public was so incalculable; it vacillated between intelligence and stupidity, sympathy and condemnation. He was too fair and just to condemn the theatre wholesale, but the incredible ignorance and lack of observation in the masses appalled him. They could not, it seemed, differentiate between the false and the true, and their sense of values was hopelessly muddled and wrong. To see bad psychology, insincerity and false situations accepted and acclaimed on the stage was too painful, but an audience would, it seemed, accept any situation, however false, provided that such a situation appealed to its vanity. That, at least, was Tchehov's opinion. He had seen it only too often.

Certainly the theatre at that time in Russia was in a bad way. Tchehov had come to the conclusion, too, that the majority of actors failed lamentably in their work. They were ignorant and unobservant. "Actors never observe ordinary people," he said. "They know nothing of country squires or tradespeople, or parsons, or civil servants, though they can represent superbly billiard markers, kept mistresses, debauched sharpers, generally all the types they observe in their visits to public houses and bachelor parties."

The theatre had really given Tchehov a bad fright. "Fiction", he said, "is a peaceful and blessed business, but dramatic writing is like a noisy, showy, impertinent and tiresome mistress." Either one had to write plays badly and impudently or else take the work as "something extremely serious and difficult".

Finally, however, it was decided that *Ivanov* should be revived, but before doing so, Tchehov polished and reconstructed the play, a task which was, as he confessed, as "difficult as buying a soldier's old trousers and trying to turn them into an evening jacket". Nevertheless, he worked on it with great enthusiasm and earnestness. "Ah, shoot me if I grow mad and do not do the work that becomes me," he wrote to a friend.

Ivanov was eventually produced in Petersburg, early in February 1889, at the Alexandrinsky Theatre, and the revival was quite successful. But the controversy over the play broke out again. Tchehov received many letters, anonymous and otherwise, criticising the piece, and one indignant member of the audience (evidently a Socialist) sent him a bitter letter of reproach, in which he declared that the play was harmful. These letters were not seriously disturbing, but Tchehov was hurt that the public should so misunderstand his work. "Ah," he wrote to a friend, "I implore you not to fall in love with the stage, please."

Yet when all was over, the young playwright was genuinely touched by the efforts of the actors. He knew that they had done their utmost to make *Ivanov* a success, and he was deeply grateful. He could not forget that Madame Strepetov had shed tears after the third act, and that "the actors had wandered about in joy like shadows". Indeed, he declared that they had all become as near and dear to him as the patients he had cured, or the children he had tutored.

It was clear, too, that the interest shown in *Ivanov* had done much to enhance his reputation as a dramatist, a fact for which he was grateful. On the other hand, the lionising which followed was distasteful. He was tired of being praised and fêted, and he longed only to get away from the admiring crowd and to live a simple country life. "To lie on the hay or catch a perch on a hook" was all he desired, and day and night he dreamed of "a little farm" where he could live in peace.

The public, however, refused to leave him alone, and in Petersburg every conceivable rumour as to his health, affections and finances was being circulated. It was said that he was going mad, that he was dying from loss of blood, and that he had married a certain lady and taken a huge dowry. These rumours, of course, were quite without foundation, but they were particularly annoying at this time as he was greatly concerned over his brother Nicolay, who was suffering from tuberculosis and was seriously ill at Soumy, where Tchehov and his family were now staying for the summer. There was no specific cure or drug for this disease in those days, and Tchehov was devoting all his spare time to the task of treating and caring for him. Indeed, as Anton was a doctor, the family apparently expected him to shoulder the entire burden. But it was fairly clear that the disease was beyond cure; Nicolay had been ill, off and on, for a long time; he was very breathless, very emaciated. Another anxiety was that there was an outbreak of diphtheria in the village, with which Tchehov was expected to deal.

The weather was so fine and warm that one could sit by the open window and listen to the hoopoes, nightingales and robins singing, and in the orchard the apple and pear trees were in bloom. But all this beauty counted for nothing in face of the tragic condition of Nicolay. In his character there was much to love and admire, but he was an extremely difficult and exacting patient, and continually grumbling and raging. To add to their troubles the village dogs howled all night and quite prevented sleep. How could any author work under such conditions? He was trying to write a play—*The Wood Demon*, but the piece grew so slowly that Suvorin had accused him of idling. The only relaxation he allowed himself, however, when he could snatch a few moments from the invalid, was an occasional short spell of fishing. At night, too, he would read Gogol to his family.

So the weeks passed, and everything that could be

done for Nicolay was cheerfully undertaken. But it was all too late. With the rapidity characteristic of this grave disease the patient "melted away like wax". It was terrible to see him suffer, but nothing, apparently, could save him. His death, however, came peacefully, and he was borne to the village church by his family, attended by torch-bearers and banners, according to the custom. On his forehead was placed a bandage on which were sacred texts and figures of saints, and a cross was put into his hand; a plate of food was set beside the coffin, and a Mass was sung by the priests. The relatives, weeping bitterly, kissed Nicolay's dead hand, the coffin was closed, and the burial took place, each mourner throwing a handful of sand into the grave.

This, the first death in the family, was a great sorrow, and over Tchehov it hung like a black cloud for weeks; even writing could not console him. He was so depressed and restless, in fact, that although his family stayed on at Soumy, he decided, at the invitation of a friend, to go away. He did not care where he went—to the Tyrol or even to Siberia. Finally he went to Odessa, where he spent a lazy holiday, and met and enjoyed the company of many charming actresses. He was trying to forget that agonising death-bed scene, and the suffering of that unhappy brother. He was trying to blot from his memory his mother's sorrow for the death of her son, but even now he could hear her pitiful weeping . . . . .

By the end of September Tchehov was back again in Moscow, writing and working, though with little enthusiasm, as now, for some reason, Moscow seemed alien and un-friendly. The men whom he had once looked upon as friends no longer seemed sincere or genuine, and "for one honest man there appeared to be twenty who were cunning and evil". Possibly this feeling was caused by his own depression. It was a fact, however, that he was now being severely criticised like any other public figure, and some of his critics insisted that he was not a great writer because his work had no unifying idea, no special philosophy. "Why did he not make himself clear?" they said. And so at last he spoke out:—

"I am not a Liberal, nor a Conservative, nor a meliorist nor an indifferentist. I should like to be a free artist and nothing more, and I grieve that God has not given me the power to be one. I hate falsehood and lying in all their aspects . . . I look upon trademarks and labels as prejudices. My Holy of Holies is the human body, health, mind, talent, inspiration, love and the most absolute freedom, freedom from violence and falsehood in whatever form they may be manifested. This is the programme I would follow if I were a great artist."

In the meantime, work was essential, and by the second week in October he was concentrating once more on his play *The Wood Demon*. This had been left unfinished owing to Nicolay's illness and death, but M. Solovzov, who had taken the Bronnikovsky Theatre in Moscow, was interested in the play and offered the author a thousand roubles if he could finish it in ten days' time. Tchehov therefore started at once to re-write the piece, and his brother Michael copied for him, the copies, as they were finished, being despatched by messenger to the censor at Petersburg.

There is no doubt that *The Wood Demon* was written in far too great a hurry, and when Tchehov was unwell. But Solovzov was apparently satisfied with the play, and it was produced on December 27th, 1889. As might have been expected, it was a failure. It had been rushed through, and the casting of the parts was bad. The co-lessee of the theatre, for instance, had insisted on playing the part of the young heroine, but she was a stout woman who looked anything but juvenile, and unfortunately the actor who played the opposite lead was very thin. His love-making, therefore, seemed a little incongruous. The glow of the forest fire, too, was so intense that it caused laughter amongst the audience. On such apparently unimportant trifles does the fate of a play sometimes depend.

Tchehov was bitterly disappointed at the failure of the piece, and eventually it was taken off. He vowed, in fact, that he had finished with the theatre, and declared that he had failed lamentably. "I want passionately to hide myself somewhere for five years", he wrote to Suvorin, "and engage in a serious detailed work. I must teach myself, learn everything from the beginning, since as a writer I am a complete ignoramus. I must write with all my conscience, with feeling, with gusto, write not five folios a month but one folio in five months." Soon he would be thirty, yet he felt that he had only progressed as far as a man of twenty-two.

This was grossly unfair to himself, yet absolutely typical, for Tchehov could not possibly regard his work as merely a means of making a livelihood. He believed that the influence of the printed word was far-reaching; it was so vast that it could not be estimated, and as he had chosen this profession he must endeavour to be worthy of the talents he had inherited. To his light-minded contemporaries, no doubt, he was a crank, but their opinions did not concern him; he could only do his duty as he saw it.

Chapter 11

Journey to Sahalin

THE failure of *The Wood Demon* meant more to Tchehov than he cared to admit, for he was certain that the fault lay with himself. It seemed that he had failed to convince even so small an audience as a theatre audience that his work had any value. Therefore, he must read, work, study and prove himself again. For this purpose he felt that he ought to undertake some important task, something which would be a real test of his staying power and strength.

He suddenly decided, therefore, to go to Siberia to visit the penal settlement on the island of Sahalin. There he would find out for himself the exact state of things, and endeavour to expose what he saw. Sahalin was apparently a place of intolerable sufferings. "We have debased in our prisons millions of people; we have debased them at random, without thinking, barbarously," he said.

But this project, as he soon realised, was not a simple one. Sahalin is situated on the west side of the sea of Okhotsk, and a journey of 11,000 versts across Siberia was as difficult and hazardous an undertaking in those days as one could possibly conceive, for the Siberian railway did not then exist and most of the journey would have to be done with horses. Nevertheless Tchehov was determined to go, and from his brother Michael (who was studying treatises on the management of prisons and penal settlements in preparation for taking his degree in Law) Tchehov borrowed every possible document on Sahalin. He read them with increasing horror. It seemed that thousands of men had been sent there to rot in prisons and had been destroyed, body and soul. Men had been driven through the cold in iron chains for thousands of miles, and as a result of their terrible hardships they had become depraved, criminal and diseased. This appalling state of affairs had existed for years, yet it seemed that no one cared. Actually, however, some good work had already been done in Sahalin, twenty-five or thirty years previously, and the men who had worked there had achieved much in the way of reform for the prisoners.

Tchehov discussed his project with Suvorin at the first opportunity, but the great publisher was strongly opposed to the idea, chiefly, it seems, because he feared that his friend's health would not stand the strain of the long journey. He insisted that Tchehov would be wasting his time and talent in going, for Sahalin was of no use and of no interest to anyone.

But Tchehov had made up his mind. He was determined to get first-hand knowledge of convict colonization and he was convinced that Sahalin was the only place (with the exception of Australia and Cayenne) where this was possible. Although he did not pretend or hope that his expedition would make any valuable contribution to either literature or science (for he felt that he lacked the requisite knowledge, the time and the talent), yet he did hope to do something for medical science. On his return he planned to write of all he had seen, and possibly—no easy task in Russia at that time—create some public interest in the island and achieve something in the way of reform of the penal system. "If I succeed", said Tchehov, "then glory be to God! If not, then it cannot be helped."

His plan was to leave Moscow in April, when the river Kama would be open. This meant that he could devote the whole of February and March to reading, making notes and generally preparing himself for his task. And now that he had really decided to go he could dream and think of nothing but Sahalin. All day and every day he read and wrote, and the more he read the more he realised the immensity of the work he was about to undertake. He feared, also, that after Kennan's revelations of the penal system in Siberia he would be refused permission to visit the prisons in Sahalin. That, however, remained to be seen

Tchehov intended to finance this expedition himself, and after estimating the amount of his resources he found that it would just be possible. But in March the *Severny Vestnik*, a paper to which he had contributed for some years, suddenly ceased publication. This paper had been paying Tchehov in instalments and he had hoped to receive a lump sum from them, which would help him with his journey. The excellent Suvorin, however, came to his assistance, and advanced him fifteen hundred roubles.

By the second week in April Tchehov had made all his preparations. He had equipped himself with a fur coat, a waterproof leather coat, big boots, stores of food and—"for cutting sausages and hunting tigers"—a large knife! But his application for a free pass from the Head of the Prison Administration was refused. Here was an unexpected setback. Tchehov, however, was not deterred and he decided to go simply as a newspaper correspondent. There would probably be some conflict with the authorities before he reached Sahalin, but he must take that risk.

Tchehov wrote to Suvorin before he set out, and realising that the journey was bound to be difficult and dangerous, asked him, if he should never return, to see that all his property was handed over to his sister, Marie, who would pay his debts, if any. To dear Lika, a woman friend, he sent a photograph: "To the nicest of creatures, from whom I now run away to Sahalin, and who has scratched my nose. I warn wooers and admirers to wear thimbles on their noses. *P.S.* Neither this inscription nor the exchange of photographs binds me to anything!"

On the third week in April, Tchehov left Moscow and started for Sahalin. His mother accompanied him as far as the Troitska Monastery, where she was to stay in his absence, and his sister came as far as Kostroma. Then by steamer he proceeded down the Volga.

That wide and lovely river was not yet at its best, but the banks were already green, and the monasteries and white churches were bathed in sunshine. Gulls hovered over the water, and now and then the sound of a shepherd's horn was heard.

By April 24th he was sailing down the river Kama, but the weather had turned cold and he arrived at Ekaterinburg accompanied by rain, hail and snow. Ekaterinburg was a poor town, and horribly noisy. "All night long they beat on sheets of iron at every corner here," wrote Tchehov. "One needs a head of iron not to go crazy with the incessant clanging."

He discovered that the first steamer to Tomsk was due to leave on the 18th May, which meant that he would have to drive across Siberia with horses, and he was advised not to use the posting service but to take a private driver instead. Eventually he was given a basket-work chaise driven by two horses, and, feeling "rather like a goldfish in a cage", he drove out of Tyumen on the 3rd of May, to start his long adventurous drive across the plain of Siberia. In Moscow he had been warned against dangerous escaped convicts and bandits; he would almost certainly be robbed or murdered. But the risk must be taken. He intended to visit Sahalin, and nothing would deflect him from his purpose now.

The weather was cold, with a piercing wind, and in places the snow had not yet melted; ice still covered many of the lakes, snow fell occasionally, and at night there were severe frosts. He wore his fur coat and two pairs of breeches, yet was quite unable to keep warm.

The plain of Siberia, with its alternating rivers and forests, was the most desolate wilderness imaginable, and the only travellers he met were occasional tramps, plodding along with their packs, and their pots and pans. These men, apparently, roamed all over the plain of Siberia, and although they had been known to murder beggars or brother exiles they did not molest travellers.

The posting stations were from twenty to forty versts

apart, according to the distance between the villages.
What a relief it was, therefore, to reach a village, with food,
warmth and lights, after driving for many hours! While
the horses were being changed Tchehov would curl up in
some corner and sleep. Yet a moment later—or so it
seemed to the weary traveller—the driver would rouse him,
saying "Get up, friend; it is time to start".

At about five in the morning the chaise would stop at
a hut, and Tchehov would drink tea. And while he did so
he would talk with the peasant women, whom he found
friendly and entertaining. They had a great sense of
humour, and were as strong, as clever and as tall as their
husbands, so—unlike the Russian peasant women—they
were never beaten or ill-used. Sometimes, when their
husbands were away from home, they would act as drivers.

The Siberian peasants, with whom occasionally he
spent the night, were clean and simple folk, and he was
much impressed by their kindliness, hospitality and industry.
They lived in wooden huts, but the beds were good, the
floors were painted or covered with home-made linen rugs,
and the rooms he visited were orderly and tidy. The food,
however, was poor, and there was a depressing lack of
variety about it; only the home-made bread was good.

Tchehov was surprised to find that there were churches
and schools everywhere in Siberia and it was obvious that
a real effort was being made to improve the lot of the
peasant. But it was depressing to discover that there were
neither hospitals nor doctors. The doctoring was done by
"feldshers", and bleeding and cupping were their favourite
methods of treatment.

For the first three days of his journey Tchehov ached
from head to foot with the incessant shaking and jolting of
the carriage. The roads were appalling, and towards
evening, when they began to freeze, the deep mud was
transformed into hard lumps. The chaise rocked and
swayed from side to side; it bumped, it stuck, it almost fell
to pieces. The horses staggered and fell, but were lashed up
again and again. How the drivers cursed and swore! And

even Tchehov's good humour sometimes almost deserted
him. But when "the going" was good, what an interesting
country it was! Snipe and woodcock fluttered about in the
birch copses, and hares stood on their hind legs and pricked
up their ears as the chaise flew past. On the lakes and
pools, and flying overhead, were swarms of ducks, wild
geese, cranes and swans.

The cold weather continued, and there were frosts
every night, but Tchehov's health improved daily. His
cough vanished and his appetite was good. He soon grew
accustomed to the incessant driving, and though at first he
was unable to sleep in the daytime owing to the rough
roads, after a time he discovered that it was possible to
sleep a little, now and then. On one occasion, however,
he was extremely thankful to be awake, for in the dim
light just before dawn he suddenly woke to the realisation
that a post-cart with three horses was bearing down upon
the chaise at full gallop. Tchehov's driver barely had time
to turn to the right when immediately behind came another
cart, also at full speed. It was impossible to avoid a collision
and in another instant there was a crash, the "horses were
mixed up in black mass, the chaise was rearing in the air",
and Tchehov was flung to the ground with all his luggage
on top of him. With great presence of mind he leapt up,
just as a third troika came dashing towards them.

There was a great uproar, and a "storm of ferocious
abuse on either side". When this had subsided, the drivers
suddenly remembered their passenger. Miraculously,
Tchehov was not hurt, but the horses and carts were in a
bad way; the traces were torn, the shafts were broken, the
yokes were strewn all over the road. How the drivers
blasphemed and swore! Standing amongst that rough
turbulent crew, whose oaths he barely understood, Tchehov
experienced such solitude and homesickness as he had
never felt before in his life.

Chapter 12

Across Siberia

A FTER five or six days driving, the weather changed, and torrential rain fell incessantly, night and day. The frozen roads became tracks of deep melting snow, and one evening, on reaching the posting station, Tchehov was told that it was impossible to proceed any further as the countryside was flooded and many of the bridges had been carried away. Knowing that the drivers habitually tried to frighten travellers with the elements, he refused to wait, but ordered the man to harness the horses. However, they had not driven more than three versts when they saw that the land on both sides of the river Irtysh was almost completely covered with great lakes, and many roads had disappeared. Nevertheless, they drove on through the floods, though at each bridge Tchehov was obliged to get out of the chaise (an uncovered one) to hold the horses, which had to be led over, one at a time.

They continued thus until dark, but soon it was obvious that the whole countyside was under water, and when at last they reached the last strip of land which separated the Irtysh from the lake, the ferryman refused to ferry them over; he declared that the weather was far too wild. The only course was to spend the night in a hut on the lake, at the edge of the Irtysh. The wind howled in the darkness, the water gurgled mournfully against the banks, and there was a penetrating dampness in the air which chilled him through and through. Was it wise or even safe to continue? He was warned that what lay ahead of him was probably worse. Yet to turn back now and confess that his tour had been a failure was unthinkable. Suvorin was expecting an account of his journey, and also many articles on Sahalin.

At all costs, therefore, he must press on.

Fortunately by the 11th of May the floods had subsided sufficiently to enable him to continue his journey.
But the cold was still terrible, night and day, and his
progress became a desperate life-and-death struggle with
the flooded rivers. He had to make use of boats time and
time again, he had to wade through deep mud, and sometimes he had to walk for miles. Nevertheless, he did at
length reach Tomsk.

Here he was strongly advised to stay until the rains
were over. In any case steam navigation on Lake Baikal
did not begin until the 10th of June, and the time of waiting
could be spent in writing an account of his experiences.
Told in retrospect his adventures were more amusing than
terrifying, and the journey had been less difficult than he
had anticipated. He felt, in fact, that in spite of the floods
his expedition had been successful. Only on one matter
had he made a wrong estimate—the journey had cost him
far more than he had anticipated. Owing to the floods he
had had to pay the drivers double and sometimes treble
rates. Also, the merest necessities were very expensive, and
the further he went the dearer everything became.

For the next stage of his journey (to Irkutsk, a distance
of 1,500 versts) he was advised to buy a trap, which he was
told could probably be sold when his horse journey ended,
at Sryetensk. So the trap was purchased (at a cost of 130
roubles) and he set off once more, driving incessantly. The
weather had improved, but the roads were appalling, and
the chaise stuck continually in the deep mud and great
pot-holes. It did, indeed, break down twice, and on each
occasion it took from ten to fifteen hours to mend. The
question of food also presented some difficulty, as milk and
eggs were plentiful but little else could be obtained.

It was only after many adventures and delays that
Tchehov at last reached Irkutsk, from which town he crossed
Lake Baikal by steamer. And this was a delightful experience; the lake was wonderfully transparent, and the
colour of the water was the most exquisite turquoise blue.

The banks of the lake, too, were mountainous and covered with luxurious forests. But conditions on the boat were not so happy, as most of the deck was occupied by the waggon horses, which were so wild that he felt he was travelling in a "brigands' " steamer.

At Myskan it was necessary again to hire horses and to gallop on, day and night, in order to reach Sryetensk to catch the steamer. There was, in fact, no time to think of either sleep or meals, and the drivers drove like madmen. Their horses, too, were "regular vipers", and while the trace-horse was being harnessed it had to be hobbled, as the moment it was set free it went flying "as if the devil were after it".

With these fearsome steeds Tchehov actually covered two hundred versts in twenty-four hours, arriving just in time to board the steamer. But again fate was against him, as on the 21st June the steamer ran upon a rock, stove several holes in her sides and settled on to a sandbank. Repairs were duly put in hand and apparently completed, but the following day more holes were discovered, and the pumping and patching began again. Many of the passengers appeared to be enjoying the situation, for when Tchehov grumbled at the delay they asked laughingly, "Why, aren't you all right here?"

At this stage of the proceedings another steamer, the "Vestnik", approached from the opposite direction, and owing to the operations of the "Yermak", was unable to proceed. The "Vestnik" was crowded with passengers, amongst whom, to the great delight of the schoolgirls, were many naval and military officers. The bands began to play, friendships and flirtations started, and the schoolgirls were heard to say that they hoped the steamer would never be repaired!

But what amazed Tchehov was the fact that these people were not afraid, as in Russia, to voice their opinions, for apparently there was no one to arrest them, and they were already living in exile. It seemed that an escaped convict could travel freely on the steamer without any fear

F

of the Captain betraying him to the authorities. In fact, "the lowest convict could breathe more freely on the Amur than the highest General in Russia".

Many of the passengers were gold miners; they grew rich quickly, and as quickly became poor again. The exiles, and even the priests, followed the same occupation, and some of these miners were highly intelligent. The Chinese passengers, too, were very entertaining. They would sit on deck and sing queer mournful songs in their thin falsetto voices, quite unconscious of the laughter and notice they provoked. But how good natured, how naive they were! And what delightful manners they had! Their courtesy was charming.

Within a few days the repairs to the steamer were completed, and the "Yermak" continued her journey down the Amur. Here the scenery was so wild, luxuriant and beautiful that Tchehov was almost "giddy with ecstasy". He saw "a million gorgeous landscapes".

His journey was now coming to an end, and in retrospect it was really a remarkable one, for he had driven with horses more than four thousand versts, and his horse-journey had lasted two months. Few men, surely, had driven so far in so short a time. Yet the rest and the fresh air had definitely benefited his health; he was wonderfully fit.

But before he reached Sahalin he witnessed an incident which greatly distressed him. On board the steamer which took him to the island was a convict who had murdered his wife. The man was in chains, and his little daughter, a child of six years, accompanied him. She followed him wherever he went, holding on to his fetters. The convict was guarded by a soldier with a gun, and at night the child slept with the convicts and soldiers, all in a heap. Tchehov was afraid for that child, and her pale drawn face haunted him for days.

Chapter 13

Work in Sahalin

ON July 11th, by way of Vladivostok, Tchehov reached Sahalin, and was received by the local administration very kindly. He began his work at the Northern end of the Island, but he found that Galkinvrasskoy (the Prison Administrator to whom he had originally applied for a pass) had sent no word of his intended visit. The other influential persons to whom he had applied for help had not attempted to prepare the way for him, either. Therefore he was obliged to proceed on his own initiative.

His first step was to make the acquaintance of the Sahalin General, Kononovitch. Tchehov then made a complete tour of the settlements, and interviewed every convict and settler. At the same time he made a careful and detailed census. It was obvious, however, that in order to return to Moscow before the winter he would have to work quickly, so every morning he rose at five and worked until late at night. Determined to see everything, he visited all the celebrities and went down the mines, he talked to men who were chained to trucks, and was present at a flogging—an incident which robbed him of sleep for many nights.

But although he had come to Sahalin prepared for the very worst conditions, yet he was horrified by the misery, poverty and immorality that now surrounded him. The condition of the young people and children was particularly bad. He saw starving children, many of whom were blind, and most of whom were filthy and covered with eruptions. He saw girls of thirteen who were already living in prostitution, and girls of fifteen already pregnant. Churches and schools existed only "on paper", actually the children were

educated only by their environment and the convict surroundings, for vice and poverty had become part of their
everyday lives.

On one occasion Tchehov went into a hut, and
finding that the occupants were not at home, began to
question a small boy. The boy was round-shouldered and
bare-footed.

"What is your father's second name?" asked Tchehov.

"I don't know" answered the boy.

"How is that?" asked Tchehov. "You live with your
father and don't know his name."

"He is not my real father" said the boy. "He is
living with mother."

"Is your mother married or a widow?" asked Tchehov.

"A widow. She followed her husband here."

"What has become of her husband, then?" asked
Tchehov.

"She killed him" replied the boy shortly.

"Do you remember your father?"

"No, I don't. I am illegitimate. I was born when
mother was at Kara." (Another penal settlement.)

Tchehov also attended a funeral, and the callousness
with which the ceremony was carried out struck him as so
deplorable that he made a special note of what took place.
It was a cold, damp day. Beside the newly-dug grave stood
four convict bearers. There also present the dead
woman's lodger (a Circassian), and a convict woman who
had come out of pity and brought the dead woman's two
children, one a baby, and the other a boy of four. The
convicts were actually laughing as the funeral proceeded,
and seemed utterly indifferent to the fate of the two little
orphans. The small boy seemed to take only the faintest
interest in the proceedings. When at last they began to fill
in the grave, Tchehov said to him, "Alyoshka, where is your
mother?" The child laughed, waved his hand "with the
air of a gentleman who has lost at cards", and said, "They
have buried her." The convict bearers laughed, too, and
thereupon the Circassian turned to Tchehov and asked

what he was to do with the children, as it was not his duty
to feed them.

This attitude amongst the inhabitants of the island
was only too common, and as Tchehov came face to face
with such dreadful callousness day after day, something
like despair took possession of him. It seemed hopeless to
imagine that anything could be done for such people, for
brutality and poverty had apparently crushed all endeavour,
all sense of honour and responsibility. Most of the women—
who composed about twelve per cent of the population—
had been transported for crimes of passion. "I'm here for
my husband," they would say casually, or "I'm here for my
mother-in-law," and the Governor of the island apparently
regarded such women as useful for only one purpose, as he
said, in addressing a group of men (settlers), "I shall see
that you get your fair share of women". Apparently a
comforting and necessary assurance!

Human dignity, in fact, and a woman's natural
feelings of modesty and shame were not taken into consideration at all, the belief being that such feelings had been
destroyed by her disgrace, or at any rate during the time
she had spent in the different prisons on her way to Sahalin.
On the other hand, many women convicts told Tchehov
that their lives with the settlers were much happier than
their former lives with their husbands, because, being
unmarried, they were free to leave at any time; they were
therefore treated with more consideration and respect. It
seemed, however, that a woman's freedom to leave a
settler was generally earned only after several beatings
with the birch.

In spite of the disheartening nature of his task Tchehov
went steadily on, and in two months' time he had interviewed all the prisoners in the north of Sahalin and had
actually registered 10,000 prisoners and settlers. He then
sailed to the South of the Island, where he followed the
same procedure as before. The weather, fortunately, was
warm and bright, and the authorities gave him every
assistance. A month later he had finished. But Sahalin,

for whose sake he had travelled some thousands of miles in storm and flood, had exacted a heavy penalty for her secrets, and he was weary and depressed. For the past three months his only society had been that of convicts and persons whose entire conversation was of penal servitude and the lash. Now he longed only to get away from it all; he was unashamedly homesick. "When I remember that I am ten thousand versts away from my world, I am overcome with apathy," he wrote to Suvorin. "It seems that I shall not be home for hundreds of years."

But to return to Russia now was impossible, as cholera was raging in Vladivostok, Japan and Shanghai, and all vessels were in quarantine; steamers were not calling at Sahalin. How long this would last no one could foresee, and there was also a very real danger of the cholera reaching the island, in which case he might be forced to spend the winter there. A grim thought!

So September passed, and signs of autumn crept over the island. Snow had fallen on the mountains, and the mornings were sharp with hoar frost. No steamers arrived, and even news of the cholera was hard to come by, for at the station of Korsakovo, where Tchehov was living for the time being, there was neither telegraph nor post. Every day, therefore, he walked down to the harbour and gazed over the sea, and each time he came back disappointed. He had booked his passage on the "Petersburg", but no one knew when she was expected. And no one seemed to care, either.

Tchehov waited patiently for six days, and at last he was wakened one night by the siren of a steamer. Here, surely, was the longed-for release. So dressing quickly he hurried with a lantern down to the harbour. Other people followed, and clustered together, they strained their eyes through the darkness. Yes, there really was a steamer some way out, but not, alas, the "Petersburg". This was the "Baikal", and Russia, apparently, was as far off as ever. Would he ever get away from this fearful island?

Yet even epidemics come to an end at last, and on

the 10th of October the welcome news reached Sahalin that the cholera in Vladivostok and Japan had abated. Three days later the "Petersburg" arrived, and Tchehov was able to leave. It was, indeed, a blessed relief, and to be out on the sparkling sea again was like emerging from a black nightmare into the light of day.

The voyage home by way of India and the Suez Canal was a delightful one, and he was utterly charmed with Ceylon; it was "an earthly paradise". Here he rode on the railway, saw all the sights, and gazed at palm forests and bronze women to his heart's content. But by December 9th he was at home again, sitting at his table and already making plans for the book on Sahalin he intended to write. As an author he certainly had some authority, and with the help of Suvorin he intended to do all in his power to assist the wretched human beings on that hellish island. The book would be heavily censored and would have to be written with circumspection and the greatest care for detail. Nothing must be overstressed or exaggerated, and his experiences must be set down calmly; otherwise he would be accused of propaganda and his case would fall to the ground. He felt that the task, too, was urgent; the book must be written soon, while the impressions were vivid in his mind. He would have to fit it in with the rest of his work, but time must be found, for "Sahalin" should be regarded as a serious social task.

Chapter 14

Continental Holiday

IT was good to be back in Moscow again, and—thanks to the long sea voyage which had definitely benefited his health—Tchehov was an excellent spirits. Now he had time to think over his experiences in Sahalin and to see them in the right proportion. Would they, perhaps, with time, lose their harsh outline and assume a softer and kinder tone? On the contrary, the more he thought about the island the darker the picture grew, and looking back on it from the security of Moscow he could only describe it as "a perfect hell". And of the Primorsky Region and Russia's Eastern Sea coast, "with its fleet, its problems and its Pacific dreams altogether" Tchehov had only one impression— "Its crying poverty; poverty, ignorance and worthlessness, that might drive one to despair. One honest man for ninety-nine thieves, that are blackening the name of Russia."

All this he passionately desired to discuss with Suvorin; his soul was in a "ferment". Suvorin, therefore, begged Tchehov to come to Petersburg. So in January, when the articles on Sahalin were finished, the two friends met again. Petersburg welcomed him warmly and once more Tchehov was fêted and flattered as the literary lion of the day. Parties were given in his honour, and visitors and letters arrived almost hourly. Yet after a few days he was firmly convinced that all was not well. There were rumours, quite without foundation, to the effect that there was some sinister purpose behind his visit to Suvorin, and in certain circles Tchehov became aware of a vague atmosphere of ill-feeling towards him. "They feed me with dinners and pay me the vulgarest compliments and at the same time they are ready to devour me," he said. It seemed, indeed, that people were ready to "tear him to pieces with envy and ill-will".

Life in Petersburg and Moscow, too, after his Sahalin labours, seemed petty, bourgeois and dull. Men and women were concerned solely with their own little lives. He was disappointed, too, to find that he could not settle down to any serious work in Petersburg. He had hoped to write, but visitors gave him no peace. No sooner had he sat down at his desk and arranged his papers than the bell rang and a visitor was announced. Everyone wished to discuss Sahalin, but they stayed so long, they talked endlessly, and they asked innumerable questions. He appreciated their interest in his expedition, but it was essential that he should work, as in his absence family debts had accumulated.

He decided, therefore, to return to Moscow, where he began almost at once to write. How delightful, now, was the thought of the coming summer! In another few months he would be able to go into the country; he was already making plans. He would find some pretty spot where good fishing could be obtained, and there, with his family and a few friends he would be able to relax. He would rise very early, write before breakfast, and get through a mountain of work; that would leave time for amusements, talks, parties, picnics, and fishing. "I long to prepare my fishing tackle," he wrote to Suvorin; and Suvorin may well have smiled at this letter, for the month was February, and Moscow was piled high with snow.

During his stay in Petersburg Suvorin had announced that he was planning a trip to Italy and was very anxious for Tchehov to join the party. But Tchehov had pointed out that he could not possibly afford an expensive holiday. He was at that time living "more frugally than a mouse", but a trip with Suvorin, who always travelled expensively, meant that Tchehov would have to borrow at least a thousand roubles, a sum that would be difficult to repay. Suvorin, however, insisted that he was only too willing to lend the money and that the debt would simply be an advance on future payments. Besides, it was essential for Tchehov to escape the Russian winter; the doctors had consistently advised it. It was essential, also, for him to travel, and see Europe.

Tchehov held out for some weeks, but the idea of going abroad was irresistible, so finally he decided to go. Indeed, he might never again have such an opportunity. "My soul is leaping with delight," he wrote to Suvorin.

The party began their tour by a visit to Vienna, and Tchehov was immediately enchanted by this delightful city, with its exquisite churches, magnificent shops and beautiful and elegant women; everything completely fascinated him. And how good it was to find oneself in a country where it was possible to read anything, and to speak one's mind without fear of the consequences! Ah, freedom! What a glorious thing it was! But although he was enjoying these new and delightful experiences, he did not forget his people at home. "I miss you all", he wrote, "and indeed I am conscience-stricken at deserting you all again . . . Don't forget me with my many transgressions. I embrace you. I bless you."

On March 22nd Tchehov and Suvorin arrived in Venice, a Venice that was bathed in sunshine, and Tchehov was quite intoxicated with the place; everything delighted him—the architecture, the bird-like and graceful gondolas, the cathedral, the people. The "brilliance", life, joy, and freedom were something he had never dreamed of. "For us poor, oppressed Russians," he wrote, "it would be easy to go out of our minds here in a world of beauty, wealth and freedom. One longs to remain here for ever . . ." To see the tiny house where Desdemona lived affected him profoundly, and he was charmed by the beauty of the evenings in Venice. How lovely were the gondolas hung with lanterns, flitting to and fro along the canals! And the superb singing moved him to tears. "My God," he wrote, "one might almost die of the strangeness of it." He crept into the churches, where Italian women knelt with bowed heads; he listened to the wonderful organs, he stared at pictures and sculptures to his heart's content. And it seemed to him that the air was full of the vibration of church bells. He was deeply impressed and touched, too, on visiting the tombs of Canova and Titian, by the fact that great artists were buried "like Kings in churches". "Here", he said, "they do not despise Art, as with us."

But his enthusiasm was a little quenched two days later when the weather turned wet and the skies overcast. For Venice without the sun is robbed of much of its charm. The canals no longer sparkled and glittered in the sunlight, and the gondoliers, sensitive to the dreary day, forgot to sing. He and Suvorin, therefore, went on to Bologna, and from thence to Florence, where they stayed until the end of March. From there they went to Rome, where Suvorin took a salon in what was once the Palace of Cardinal Conti. But by this time Tchehov's stamina had come to an end. Strolling about the Vatican he declared that his legs were made of "cotton wool". They would barely support him.

After Rome came Pompeii, and here it was essential to see all that was to be seen. No shirking allowed! He therefore rode on horseback to the foot of Vesuvius, and then climbed for three and a half hours through "ashes, mountains of lava, solid waves of molten minerals, etc." It was an "agonising climb", and by the time he reached the crater, which he thought "very terrible", he was quite exhausted. "I believe in hell now," he said.

Monte Carlo came later, and although he thought the Casino "rather like . . . a fine den of thieves", he tried his luck at the tables. It was his first experience of gambling and at first he won, but finally, in spite of a system worked out by himself and Suvorin's son, he lost about 540 francs. "So there it is," he wrote to his brother. "You will say, of course 'What a mean thing to do! We are so poor while he plays roulette.' Perfectly just, and I give you permission to slay me. But I personally am much pleased with myself. Now I can tell my grandchildren that I have played roulette and know the feeling which is excited by gambling." He was, indeed, quite unrepentant, although he had no desire to repeat the experiment.

From Monte Carlo the party went on to Nice, where they visited the Russian church. And here he suddenly realised that Easter was not far distant. It was his first Easter away from home, and he felt sad and homesick for Russia. Indeed, he had intended to be back in time to spend the festival with his family; now it would not be possible. So he begged them all to remember him in their prayers.

Chapter 15

Holiday at Bogimovo

THE summer which followed the European tour was spent as usual in the country, and for this holiday Tchehov rented an old manor-house at Bogimovo for himself and his family. The house, which stood in a large park, belonged to the time of Catharine the Great, and there was a magnificent garden, a river and a mill. The weather was fine, the month was May, and nightingales sang continually.

As his study Tchehov used the large pillared hall, from which there was a charming view of the long avenue of lime trees, and in the distance a white, two-storied house, old, desolate and probably falling to pieces. It stood in a grove of dark fir trees, and a group of green willows was set against the terraced courtyard. It was all very romantic, and in the evening, when the warm light from the setting sun quivered upon the treetops, the place was bathed in a melancholy beauty. It was the house of his dreams, and he longed passionately to buy it, though such a plan, at the moment, was out of the question.

Life at Bogimovo was delightful, and Tchehov and his party were in excellent spirits. They arranged picnics and excursions, explored the beautiful woods, played charades in the evenings and discussed philosophy by the hour. Masha painted, Tchehov's father talked of bishops and prayed interminably, Ivan fished, and Michael caught frogs with which to feed Tchehov's pet mongoose. The landscape painter Levitan—a close friend of Tchehov's— was also of the party, and his raptures over the light on the river, the superb sunsets, the exquisite dawns, the moon shining on the cornfields, etc., etc., were highly infectious.

He was extremely talented, but no one could possibly say what he would do next, and his hectic love affairs were both diverting and alarming. Beauty in women could not be resisted, and he fell in and out of love with such rapidity and anguish that he was sometimes near to suicide. He did, indeed, once attempt to shoot himself but was unsuccessful; the bullet merely grazed his forehead. His heart, however, seemed to mend quickly. Shooting birds was one of his hobbies, yet he was so faint-hearted that he could not bear to put a wounded bird out of its misery.

Another guest was a zoologist named Wagner, who spent his time experimenting with ladybirds and spiders. "When he has finished with spiders he will begin on fleas which he will catch on his aunt," said Tchehov.

And last, but not least, there was the charming and lovely Lika Misinov, a friend of the family. Tchehov was very fond of Lika. "Enchanting, amazing Lika!" But apparently it was impossible for him to be serious, for when she had gone he wrote to her:—"When you bedewed my right shoulder with your tears (I have taken out the spots with benzine), and when slice after slice you ate our bread and meat, we greedily devoured your face and head with our eyes. Ah, Lika, Lika, diabolical beauty!" And he added, "When you are at the Alhambra with Trofimov I hope you may accidentally jab out his eye with your fork!" He insisted later that he loved her "passionately like a tiger" and he offered her his hand. But the postscript was rather surprising:—"Answer me by signs. You do squint!" In the end he declared that she was a darling and he sent her a thousand kisses.

The mongoose was a very amusing creature. It broke crockery with unfailing regularity, but nevertheless it was a great favourite. And when suddenly it escaped into the woods, the whole party were in dismay. They searched frantically everywhere, but the mongoose had vanished. It was lost for eighteen days, but was found at last by some sporting dogs. It had grown fat. "Such is the effect of freedom," said Tchehov. "Yes, my dear sir," (to Suvorin) "freedom is a grand thing."

Eventually Suvorin paid a visit to Bogimovo, and again the two men fished and resumed their interminable talks on Literature. But Tchehov got through a good deal of work, too, and by the end of July he had paid off most of his debt. He was also busy on his Sahalin book, but he knew that the censor would cast a strict eye upon his work before it could be published, so although there were times when he longed to sit over it for three or even five years, yet in moments of doubt he almost hated the book; he was chiefly concerned in attacking life sentences and the laws dealing with exiles (the latter being "fearfully out of date and contradictory"), but the penal system in Russia was so inflexible and so bound up with the whole harsh system of government that he often despaired of achieving anything in the way of reform. In the meantime, those poor wretches in Sahalin were still living and suffering. In his mind's eye he could see them now, the desperate, exhausted men, browbeaten, terrorised and devoid of hope. The children, too, in their rags and filth, haunted him; many of them had become depraved beyond redemption, and their health problems were awful to contemplate. But most of all he was concerned for the shrill, unhappy, hard-faced women and their miserable offspring. What hope could there be for these people? In their terrible isolation they had been ignored for years. And probably now it was too late; the problem was too vast. Indeed, what a lot Russia had to answer for! What an evil system it was which created such conditions for humanity! . . . Yes, Sahalin was an immense problem. It would be years before he would be able to lift it from his shoulders . . . "Ah," he wrote to Suvorin, "to make haste and become an old man and sit at a big table!"

Leisure! Rest! Like all men of his type Tchehov longed for rest, to reach the green oasis which beckoned so alluringly to the tired traveller. A few steps more, and surely the hour of repose would come! Yet in the life of an artist there can be no rest; the urgency of his vision drives him on relentlessly, night and day. To create is the breath of life to him; to create is his only chance of survival. This treadmill, it is true, has its many moments of joy, even of exquisite happiness, but it is a wearing process.

Would marriage, perhaps, bring him peace? It was possible, but at the moment that was not for him; he had far too many responsibilities. Even the lovely and desirable Lika with her fair, fair hair and her laughing eyes could not persuade him to take that step. "I don't intend to get married," he wrote firmly to Suvorin. In the meantime, Lika was hopelessly in love with Tchehov, and apparently terribly unhappy because he could not reciprocate. "You know perfectly well", she wrote later, "how I feel about you, and I am not in the least ashamed to write about it. I also know that your attitude towards me is one of condescension and indifference. My dearest wish is to cure myself of the terrible state in which I am now, but it is very difficult for me to do it by myself. I implore you to help me. Please do not ask me to come and see you and do not try to see me. This means nothing to you, but it may help me to forget you . . ."

Poor, pretty Lika! She was, apparently, doomed to love tragically, for some years later she formed a liaison with Tchehov's friend Potapenko, by whom she had a child. But Potapenko was apparently a gay, lively and somewhat irresponsible young man, who finally deserted her.

Chapter 16

Famine in Russia

THE year of 1891 was a disastrous one for Russia, for an unfortunate summer—during which the rye harvest failed—was followed by a severe autumn and winter, and many districts in Russia became famine stricken. The situation, in fact, became extremely serious. Peasants with babies and young children were standing about in the villages, wailing and crying bitterly for food. "We are starving. What are we to do? Must we die?" But apparently the famine extended over a very large area, so it was essential that any scheme of relief should be organised on an immense scale. The public, however, did not trust the Administration, and many fantastic stories were being circulated; it was said that large quantities of money and food had been stolen. The Red Cross in Moscow, in particular, came in for severe criticism, and were denounced as thieves.

For this reason the public would not subscribe to the Government schemes, but various societies and individuals were anxious to start their own famine relief. Yet when the leaders of these people went to the Home Secretary to ask permission, it was curtly refused; the famine was to be dealt with only by the Red Cross and the Government. Private initiative, in fact, was suppressed from the start, and as a result many people became discouraged, others got angry, and some simply washed their hands of the whole business. Tchehov, back again in Moscow, was anxious to take part in any scheme of famine relief, but before any definite plans could be made he caught influenza from Suvorin and was ill for weeks. His lungs were affected, and it was almost two months before he was able to con-

G

sider work of any kind; everything had to be put on one side.

But by December Tchehov was again considering what he could do; he was anxious to assist in any possible way. "With all my heart and my strength I am ready to follow you and do whatever you like," he wrote to a friend.

The Government had by this time realised that a tremendous effort must be made and had therefore reluctantly agreed to allow private initiative. As a result much had already been achieved by various committees and commissions, yet matters were still in a bad way in the famine-stricken provinces. Tchehov's plan was to appeal for subscriptions through the newspapers, in order to carry out a scheme suggested by his friend Yegorov. It appeared that the peasants were selling their horses and cattle for next to nothing, and therefore there was a grave danger that the fields would not be ploughed for the spring corn, in which case there would probably be a repetition of the famine the following year. Tchehov's plan was to buy up the horses and cattle from the peasants, feed them through the winter, and then return them in the spring to their owners.

This scheme was actually established by the end of December, and they chose the province of Nizhni-Novgorod for their activities. It was a long and arduous task which demanded the utmost care and organisation.

When at last the scheme was running smoothly Tchehov's family and friends strongly urged him to take some steps towards improving his health. It was obvious that treatment was needed, and rest in such cases had always proved beneficial. But, as usual, he refused to discuss the matter seriously. He had, he said, a horror of being doctored or sounded. He agreed to "take the waters" and quinine, but apart from that there was nothing to be done; a long rest in bed was out of the question. He did, however, agree to go and live in the country as soon as possible, and as furnished houses were expensive it would be best to buy a house. But for that a large sum must be raised. He therefore resolutely shut out all visitors, refused all invitations and began to write. He worked incessantly for weeks, alone in his Moscow flat. He felt, indeed, "like a heron in the reeds", but it was inevitable.

And as he worked he dreamed of the future. Ah, for green fields and the river running at his feet! To see the fish rise and the flies dancing above the water! To lie on the grass beneath the willows, far from the noise and smoke and restlessness of Moscow! In Moscow he rarely felt well. "It seems to me", he wrote to a friend, "that I am dried and warped like an old cupboard, and that if I go on living in Moscow next year and give myself up to scribbling excesses, Gilyarovsky will read an excellent poem to welcome my entrance into that country place where there is neither sitting nor standing . . . but only lying down." Yet on good days, when he felt that his health had improved, his enthusiasm for life and literature came back. "In the summer let us each write a play," he wrote to Suvorin. "Yes, by God, why the devil should we waste our time?"

By the end of December he was in better health, his cough was less, his strength greater, he was in good spirits and there was "sunrise" in his head. There was news, too, of a country house. His agent had found what seemed a suitable place, an estate consisting of 639 acres, in two parts. The house, formerly the property of an artist, stood in its own small park, there was a long avenue of limes (Tchehov was particularly fond of these trees), there was a good garden and orchard, a pond containing carp and tench, and two miles away there was a broad river full of fish. The forest, unfortunately, had been felled, but there were three hundred acres of young copse which would certainly have grown into a wood in twenty years time.

The house, although presenting "a very stupid and naive appearance", was light and warm, and stood in a fine position. It had french windows into the garden, and a verandah. Yes, it would do. And very soon Tchehov had made up his mind to buy the place, at a cost of 14,000 roubles.

But before he took possession he was anxious to see

his famine relief actually in operation, so in January (1892)
he visited the Province of Nizhni-Novgorod.   There he
stayed for some time, and later visited Voronezh with
Suvorin.   But this latter expedition was one long irritation,
as he and Suvorin were invited to tedious, ceremonious
dinners; and this at a time when thousands of people in
Russia were starving.   Moreover, travelling with Suvorin
hampered Tchehov's independent action; he did not want
ceremony, but longed for intense personal activity.   He
would, indeed, have liked to do what Tolstoy had done in
the way of famine relief, though this was not possible.
Tolstoy was a rich landowner with great authority in
Russia.   He had, with the assistance of his family, started
soup kitchens for the peasants, and had eventually supervised the feeding of from ten to thirteen thousand people.
He had also established a hundred and twenty-four kitchens
for children, in which two or three thousand souls were
fed.   Tolstoy had done valuable work, too, in assisting the
peasants to start life again.   He had supplied them with
material for work during the winter, and with seeds and
horses with which to start work in the Spring. "Tolstoy! ah,
Tolstoy!" wrote Tchehov.   "He is not a man but a super-
man, a Jupiter."

When the famine situation in Russia had improved,
Tchehov felt justified in returning to Moscow, where he
proceeded to make final arrangements for the purchase of
the house at Melihovo.   But as he had never before owned
any property and had had little experience of business, he
found the protracted negotiations extremely wearing.   It
was all far more complicated than he had imagined.   He
had not realised, either, that in buying a house, many
additional items were added to the purchase price, such as
the cost of purchase deeds, mortgage deeds and option bills.

However, by March the new house was ready for
occupation, and he and his family moved in.   The household, apart from servants, consisted of his old parents, Marie,
Michael and himself.   The country was still in the grip of
winter when they arrived, and the roads and fields were

piled with snow. All boundaries on the estate, therefore, were obliterated, and it was impossible to estimate the extent of the property. But when the thaw came, and the snow gradually melted, fences and walls were suddenly revealed, and every day there were fresh surprises. The thaw lasted many weeks, and during that time life in Melihovo was wretchedly uncomfortable. To drive with either sledges or carts was impossible, and the cattle pined for grass and freedom. Yet at last the starlings returned, and the weather became bright and springlike.

Life at Melihovo was in many ways a new and exhilarating experience, but it had its problems. For instance, there were only three broken-down horses on the estate and not a wisp of hay, so the horses had to be fed on rye straw chopped up with an axe and sprinkled with flour. One of the horses was very vicious, and of the remaining two, one was eventually stolen by the peasants and a dead horse left in its place. So for a long time only one horse was available with which to visit patients, haul logs, and drive back and forth to the station—a distance of nine miles along a very rough road.

The peasants, too, were difficult to understand, as newcomers, especially townsfolk, were met ungraciously, and with suspicion, almost with hostility. The Tchehovs wished only to live in peace with their neighbours and to be of real use, but they were new to country life and ways, and the fact was obvious. The peasants, therefore, took every possible advantage of their ignorance. They would graze cattle on the Tchehovs' private pasture, or even in the garden, and steal mushrooms from the fields. They would bark the trees in the woods and break down fences. They had little respect for land boundaries, and when the opportunity occurred they would steal the ploughing harness, and take the new wheels from their carts and replace them with old ones.

It seemed, indeed, to the new landowners that they were regarded in the village as stupid people who had bought an estate because they did not know what to do

with their money, an idea that was far from the truth, for
Tchehov had gone to the country chiefly for his health's sake.

The mortifications caused by the peasants, in fact,
were extremely depressing, and there was no end to the
misunderstandings, petty cares and sordid anxieties. Sometimes, for instance, the Tchehovs' cattle would be driven
away to the village, impounded and then not released until
a fine had been paid. Sometimes the unscrupulous villagers
would declare that the Tchehovs had mown some piece of
grassland which did not belong to them, and as no one at
first knew the exact boundaries of the estate, the Tchehovs
were bound to take the peasants' word for it and pay
damages. Later on it was discovered that there had been
no mistake.

The peasants were obviously nervous, irritable and
suspicious, and they were still sensitive about the serfdom of
the past. If they suspected for a moment, therefore, that
they were being coerced or exploited they would say in-
dignantly, "We are not serfs now; all that is past." Allow-
ances, of course, must be made, but it was clear that much
patience was needed in order to fit into this new life, with
all its quaint customs, prejudices, conventions and senti-
ments, many of which, from long use, were sacred to the
peasants, but utterly unknown to the Tchehovs.

Another problem which had to be solved was that
the house was found to be swarming with bugs, beetles and
mice. Also, one of the maids proved to be a professional
thief; she stole almost everything she could lay her hands
on, including money. The house, too, was far from comfortable, as it sadly lacked furniture. But Tchehov had
spent all his capital on the purchase of the house and
estate, and there was nothing left for furniture.

However, the weeks passed; Tchehov wrote stories
with great industry, and soon finances improved. Alterations to the house were put in hand, painting and decorating
were started, furniture arrived, and the place began to
assume a more cheerful and comfortable appearance.
Fortunately labour in the country was cheap—if unreliable—

and it was clear that the estate had infinite possibilities. Tchehov confessed that he knew nothing of agriculture except that the earth was black, but he bought large books on farming and the management of land, and worked accordingly. Every member of the family assisted on the estate, and Tchehov himself sowed clover, planted trees, roses and bulbs, and pruned and trained his precious nurslings with his own hands. Six horses were purchased, thirty acres each of oats, rye and hay were sown, and all the field work for the spring was completed in good time. Mistakes, of course, were made, but these were rarely irremediable.

Very soon, too, Tchehov's medical services were in great demand, for doctors were extremely scarce in the district. Sick people were brought to him in carts even from twenty miles distant, and from early morning peasant women and children stood at his door waiting. Few of them could afford to pay anything for his services, but none would leave without advice or medicine.

The Russian peasants were apparently strong both in mind and body, and could endure much hardship and fatigue, but the conditions in which they lived were scarcely conducive to health. Their log houses were warm, but the internal arrangements were very primitive, and there was no sanitation and no water supply, except from wells. Cleanliness and any form of hygiene were almost unheard of, and children and adults alike all slept on the stove. Many of the women worked in the fields all day; they therefore left their young children in the care of some neighbour or older child, and the results were often tragic; young children fell into ponds and streams, they were wrongly fed, they caught "fevers" and died like flies, and many grew up dwarfed and crippled.

The peasants were extremely superstitious, too, and there were lucky and unlucky days for almost every task. They regulated their lives by the church festivals: Thus cattle were turned out, not when there was grass for them to eat, but on the 17th of April, because it was St. Stephen's

Day. Also, the peasants would begin ploughing, not when the weather was favourable, but on St. Gregory's Day, so that he might bring success to the operation. Apples, too, were not gathered when they were ripe, but on the festival of the Virgin Mary, in August.

Amongst these primitive people Tchehov worked day and night, advising, prescribing and operating; and the amount of disease and physical disability he met with was truly appalling. The infant mortality, too, was so high that his task would have discouraged all but the most optimistic doctor. He took his work very seriously, and every patient was carefully studied; that was his nature. But for some problems there seemed no remedy. How he loathed, for instance, the continual drunkenness, and the misery it caused! How he loathed the brutality of men to their wives—an old custom which died hard!

But Spring in Melihovo was really an exquisite experience. Tchehov would rise very early in the morning, while the dew was still sparkling on the flowers, the birds were twittering, and there was not a cloud in the sky. Larks were trilling in the heavens; and the garden, the meadows and the river were really beautiful at that hour. The woods were gay with the milk-white blossom of the cherry tree and the wild peach, and the larches, birches and rowan trees were frilled with fresh green.

Easter came, and the peasants were very anxious to celebrate the Festival, but although there was a small church in Melihovo there was no priest. So Tchehov and his family collected money from the parish and obtained a priest from the Davydov Monastery. The festival was duly celebrated, the Tchehovs and their guests sang the Easter service, and the peasants were delighted. It is true that many of them celebrated too well and got drunk, but nevertheless it was a happy Easter. Good relations had been established with the villagers, and when Tchehov walked through the village the peasant women would smile and make the sign of the cross. They were no longer so suspicious of "the strangers". Tchehov's old father had also found a happy niche, as he had become the village choirmaster, and the peasants seemed to understand and to accept this old man, who was so like themselves. They had a natural love of music, and from their huts the gay sound of the balalaika was frequently heard. How interesting to watch, too, were their native crafts! And one could not but admire the simple idiom of their thought and speech, which was often strikingly wise, and of great beauty.

Chapter 17

First winter in Melihovo

BUT the news that Tchehov, the celebrated author, had settled in Melihovo, soon spread, and callers came from miles around. Doctors, members of the local Zemstvos and officials of the district all came to pay their respects; it was impossible for him to avoid publicity. His plan of hiding himself in the country, in fact, was not to materialise; he was more conspicuous in Melihovo as a celebrity than in Moscow, where celebrities were common. And life in the country was frankly disappointing, for he seemed to spend half his time dealing with petty payments, and arguments over money with lazy carpenters, painters and labourers. There was no one else capable of supervising the farming, either. Yet how could he raise any real enthusiasm for the task? He was far too busy earning a livelihood for them all, to deal with the farming properly. Besides, he had suddenly realised that on such a small scale it was merely an expensive hobby; he had no faith in it.

Life, in fact, seemed hopelessly petty and mean. "My soul longs for space and height, but perforce I must spend a narrow life over scoundrelly roubles and copecks. There is nothing more banal than bourgois life with its pennies, its victuals, its absurd talks and its useless conventional virtue. My soul has wilted from the consciousness that I am working for money and that money is the centre of my activity. This gnawing feeling, added to a sense of justice, makes my authorship a contemptible pursuit in my eyes. I do not respect what I write, I am apathetic and bored with myself, and I am glad I have my medicine, which at any rate I don't practice for the sake of money."

Such was his dark mood, and as usual, all this was

poured out to Suvorin, who as a much older man, understood and loved him. Suvorin, however, had a shrewd suspicion that Tchehov's troubles were both psychological and physical. A wife, in his opinion, would have added to his happiness and peace of mind enormously. She must be, of course, the right kind of wife, yet Tchehov, with his wonderful loyalty, gentleness and affectionate nature, would have made a devoted, ideal husband.

To Tchehov, however, the issue was not quite so simple. He could never forget that his family needed not only his financial support but his protection; they relied on him utterly. He was their mainstay, their rock, their guiding star, and he had supported and protected them for so long that he could not now change their attitude, nor, indeed, his own. "I do not want to marry," he wrote to Suvorin, "nor is there the woman . . . It would bore me to fuss about with a wife. But it would not be a bad idea to fall in love . . . Not only am I weary and discontented, but I am convinced even as a doctor, that is, quite cynically, that from this life one has to expect only evil, mistakes, losses, illnesses, weakness and all sorts of abominations."

Was this merely a black mood caused by the frustrations of the new life, his own ill-health and his intellectual loneliness? It is hard to say, but whatever the cause, this depression did not last, for Levitan and other friends came to stay, and there were shooting and fishing parties. Haymaking was uproarious fun. In the meantime, the geese were thriving, and the pond was well stocked with fish. How beautiful, too, was the surrounding country, with its woods of fir and birch, its green meadows filled with flowers, and its infinite variety of wild birds! It was delightful to hear the bleat of sheep and the church bells on bright summer mornings. In the garden, which was now so prettily laid out, the swings had been put in order and new ones constructed. They were the true Russian swings which held several people, and the Tchehovs and their guests were continually lolling, swinging and indulging themselves. It was an old Russian custom, hard to break, and very soothing.

Then in the evening, when all were cosily seated round the lamp, there would be card games, and backgammon, and much laughter and talk. Tchehov, it is true, could rarely join in; he had to write. But later on, when he was too tired to continue with his work, he would come into the drawing-room and set out his patience board, one of his few relaxations.

The long summer days passed pleasantly, and he became particularly interested in the peasants as they worked in the fields. To see the smiling, vigorous, sunburnt young women cutting the rye, for instance, was an education. How he envied their strength, their merry uninhibited laughter, their zest for life, their endurance! He would often pause to watch them, and he would say, "God speed the work!" It was an old custom and he was always answered with a cheerful salutation. The very simplicity of these people, in fact, sometimes moved him to tears. When, for instance, the women were reaping and binding the rye they would place their babies in cradles which were tied to three sticks stuck in the ground. But at intervals a mother would suddenly thrust her sickle into a bound sheaf and go to one of the cradles. She would take the crying babe in her arms, and after many kisses and caresses, would sit down and feed it from the breast. It would then be put back into the cradle, and the mother would take up her sickle again with renewed energy. The work was laborious, especially in hot weather, yet how cheerfully and willingly these country peasants laboured!

Sometimes, too, one would come across a beautiful young peasant girl, moving like some strange soft-spoken goddess amongst the crowd. Her origin, probably, was obscure, yet there could be no doubt of her beauty; and miraculously she had preserved her virginity, her purity, her loveliness. Occasionally, too, one met a man equally fine—strong, courageous, frank, honourable; one of Nature's gentlemen. Such men and women were rare, but they gave heart to one's purpose. Indeed, it could never be a waste of time to write about the peasants.

But these happy summer days were apparently too good to last, for in August disquieting news arrived which upset all his calculations and for the time being made writing impossible. In the south of Russia an epidemic of cholera was raging, and every day it came nearer to Moscow. The peasants had been weakened by the famine, and the cholera could not have found more favourable conditions for its deadly work. Hundreds of persons had already died, and many thousands were desperately ill. Tchehov, as the only doctor in the district, was appealed to for advice and assistance, and the Zemstvo of Serpuhov decided to take immediate measures. It would be fatal to wait until the cholera arrived, as hospitals were few and far between. It was decided, therefore, to erect temporary hospitals, and Tchehov was asked to organise and take charge of a "section" consisting of twenty-five villages, four factories and a monastery. But what a task this was! The work involved a mass of detailed planning, and in order to get round his district he was obliged to drive all day. The country was new to him, the roads were appalling, and his carriage and horses were quite inadequate for the work. In addition, his sight was not good, and it was almost impossible for him to see to drive on a dark night. None of these things would have bothered him had he been in sound health, but unfortunately at this time he suffered from constant headaches and was quickly exhausted.

To combat the cholera, however, was a very urgent problem, and it was obvious that there was no other man in the district capable of dealing with his particular section; so Tchehov put his whole heart and soul into the task. He must follow, in fact, the peasants' frequent jibes at each other—"Never mind how you feel; get on with your work."

The first step towards the building of temporary hospitals was to collect the necessary funds, and at the moment no money was available—a common enough state of affairs in Russia. He therefore drove round the district to ask the rich landowners if they would subscribe. But how he loathed the task, for while many excellent people were giving both time and money to the cause, others who could well afford to help either deliberately ignored his appeal or were frankly indifferent. There was, for instance, a certain rich countess whom Tchehov was asked to interview in order to organise the building of temporary hospitals for her workmen. She received Tchehov as though he had come to apply for a situation. The Archimandrite at the Monastery, too, when asked how he proposed to deal with the cases which might occur at his hostel, answered haughtily, "They are persons of means who will pay you themselves."

Frankly, the task was a very unpleasant one, and to add to Tchehov's troubles there were epidemics of typhus, scarlatina and diphtheria in his district.

By October, owing to Tchehov's excellent organisation and untiring efforts, his section was all in readiness. It had two good hospitals, properly equipped, and five others. Lime, vitriol and other disinfectants he had begged from the manufacturers for all his twenty-five villages. He had prepared the peasants, too, by giving talks and lectures during the past few months.

Cholera! Cholera! The word became almost an obsession, and even in his dreams the nightmare of its approach haunted him. He realised only too well that if it came to his district it would devastate the whole area; thousands would die; there would be little hope for them. He would wake from sleep, therefore, disturbed, perhaps, by the barking of a dog, and leap from his bed thinking, "Have they come for me?" Then realising that all was well he would creep back to bed again.

By October the cases of cholera in Moscow had been reduced to fifty a week, and although on the Don there were still a thousand cases a day, nevertheless it was clear that the virulence of the disease was abating. Tchehov therefore felt he could now devote himself to the supervision of the estate. Fortunately the summer had been a splendid one, and the place had improved almost beyond recognition. Some of the outhouses had been rebuilt, flower beds had been laid out, he had sunk a well and was building a big pond. He had planted hundreds of trees and shrubs, and he had also made a new road to the station, so that it was no longer necessary to drive through the village; and last, but not least, he had bought himself a comfortable new carriage.

By the second week in October snow had fallen in Melihovo, and the fields were white. Winter was on the way, and already the frosts had started. It was Tchehov's first winter in the country, and it was something of a revelation, for blizzards sometimes raged night and day, and the wind howled and moaned through the bare branches like some unearthly maniac. In such weather people stayed at home, so there were few visitors. His sister Marie had now returned to Moscow (where she had a post), so he seemed to be surrounded only by old women, sick babies and peasants. Nothing would have induced him to confess the fact to his old parents, but he was often extremely lonely.

And soon this loneliness began to affect not only his work, but his own attitude to his work. He wondered, for instance, whether his stories were really worth writing. And what was the purpose of his art? What did it teach? What were its aims? For when one carefully considered the works of the great writers of the past it seemed to him that each one had had a purpose; those brilliant men had not excited the imagination for nothing. All had had either remote or immediate aims, and they had shewn life not only as it is, but as it might be. They had held up a shining vision before men, unattainable, perhaps, but magnificently inspiring. He himself, however, could only depict the truth as he saw it. He had believed that it was essential for an artist to be "indifferent", insisting that only those who are "indifferent" are "able to see things clearly, to be just and to work". Now, possibly, he was wrong. And not only he himself was wrong, but his contemporaries, too, were suffering from the same stagnation, the same coldness.

To Suvorin (in whom he confided most of his thoughts) he wrote:—"We have neither immediate nor remote aims, and in our souls a great emptiness. We have no politics, we do not believe in revolution, we have no God, we are not afraid of ghosts and I personally have no fear of death or blindness . . . Surely one who wants for nothing, hopes for nothing and fears nothing cannot be an artist!"

The trouble with Tchehov was that he saw all round him struggling and unhappy people who were thwarted and fettered at every turn. Many of them were persons of high aspirations, sensitive, imaginative and possessed of a real love for Russia. But there was little or no outlet for their idealistic enthusiasms. Surely if ever Russia needed a leader of thought it was at that time! Revolutionary and Terrorist measures had proved ineffectual. What was wanted, it seemed, was a new Philosophy. And if the writers and thinkers of Russia could not proclaim a Philosophy and endeavour to show how life should be lived, to whom could the people turn?

So pondered Tchehov, but fortunately this mood of dissatisfaction with himself and his work did not last. It had descended on him, partly as a result of his isolation and loneliness, and partly because he could no longer rely upon the enthusiasms of youth. These, as was inevitable, were already leaving him. What would take their place was as yet undetermined.

In the meantime, when this spiritual crisis had passed (as pass it did) there was much that was new and interesting about which to write.

Chapter 18

Second Continental Tour

THE winter of 1893 was a very severe one, with much snow. Many of the newly planted trees on the Melihovo estate were almost buried, and the snow under the windows of the house was so high that the hares which ran into the garden would stand on their hind legs and look into Tchehov's study. He was again working on his Sahalin book, a task he had long desired to complete; in November it was finished and the proofs were sent to the chief Board of Prisons.

That most convincing and original story, *The Black Monk*, was also written at this time. It was inspired by a very vivid dream in which Tchehov saw a black monk rushing across the snow-clad fields.

His isolation in the country had therefore been responsible for one or two gloomy stories, yet at the week-ends, when visitors arrived, his good spirits returned. There would be singing, games and much laughter. Tchehov was made to join in the general merriment; but sometimes he was obliged to leave the party in order to finish a story. Yet he would soon return, with a triumphant smile:—"I have written sixty copecks' worth."

During those winter months he felt drawn to people as never before, and he paid several visits to Moscow and Petersburg. Having now no flat in Moscow he stayed at an hotel, and this he much preferred. His visits passed in an endless succession of dinners and parties; he had become light-hearted, and life was good.

But when March came it seemed that the long and dreary winter would never end. It was grim, it was unbearable, and the only pleasant alternative was to go to

H

Yalta in search of sun and warmth. Here, comfortably quartered at the Hotel Russia, he stayed for a month, and his health improved rapidly. Yet he fretted at the enforced holiday, and the knowledge that he was obliged to write in order to live never left him for a single moment. He was "torn to shreds" by the constant thought of pressing and unavoidable work. "To write, write, write!" What a burden it was! "Darling Lika," he wrote to his old friend, Lika Misinov, "When you become a great singer and are paid a good salary, make me marry you and feed me at your expense so that I may do nothing."

Lika at this time was apparently having an affair with Potapenko, but her heart still yearned for her handsome doctor friend, and she had written to him at Yalta. Tchehov was determined, however, not to take her sorrowful re-criminations too seriously, and he wrote in reply, "Although you threaten that you are soon going to die, although you tease me with having rejected you, yet I thank you" (apparently for her letter.) "I know quite well that you are not going to die and that no one has rejected you." Indeed, as a doctor, Tchehov could not take her too seriously. He had treated, as patients, many neurotic and hysterical women, and he had realised that too much sympathy merely added fuel to the fire. A little good-natured teasing was the better way. Yet for old times' sake, and because Lika was such a delightful girl he was grieved that she should be unhappy. "Lika, keep well, calm and contented," he begged. "I wish you success. You are a clever thing."

In the meantime, Tchehov was not allowed to live in peace, even in Yalta, and he was asked to "dine with noble families", lunch with headmistresses, open bazaars, and visit schools and present prizes, etc. Some of these social duties he could hardly refuse, but he avoided as many as possible, knowing that his health would not stand any extra strain. He suffered painfully, sometimes for days at a time, from palpitations. "A disgusting sensation!" he called it. And yet, as a doctor, how difficult it was to have to excuse oneself because of ill-health! The better way was to force a smile to one's lips and crack a joke. He did not want the old saying to be shot at him, "Doctor, heal thyself".

He returned to Melihovo sun-burnt and much improved in health; and again he began to plan further improvements on the estate. A new bath-house was built, and also a new barn and cattle-yard. Then finally he built, in a vain effort to secure some sort of privacy for his work, a tiny lodge in the garden consisting of three rooms. To reach it one had to pass through the orchard, but when the fruit trees were in bloom it was an enchanting spot. He had insisted, at first, that this retreat was intended to accommodate the overflow of visitors, but when it was finished his family realised that Anton had secretly always intended it for his own. One room was made to serve as a study and another as a small bedroom. Here, surely, he would be secure from noise and interruptions! Yet it was not to be. For even in the garden he was never left in peace for long, as his dear old mother was extremely hospitable, and her kindness extended to all comers, including perfect strangers. Young girls, authors, doctors, members of the local Zemstvo, and distant relatives with their families all called and insisted on meeting the famous author. They followed him about, flattered him, hung upon every word he uttered, and sometimes reduced him to a state of extreme embarrassment.

This lack of privacy was apparently the price of fame, but it made his profession, at times, extremely distasteful. "I have grown disgusted with writing", he said, "and don't know what to do. I would willingly engage myself with medicine and take some post as a doctor, but I have no longer the physical elasticity for it." And he added "It is not the writing which disgusts me, but the literary entourage "from which one cannot hide, and which one carries about everywhere, as the earth carries its atmosphere".

He was not free, either, from the attentions of women who were (or imagined themselves to be) madly in love with him. There was, for instance, Madame Avilov, the author, who was in love with him for years. She was a married woman with a family, but she had constantly sought him out. She had written to him continually, and finally persuaded herself that he was in love with her. She read a double meaning into every word he spoke, and had made herself believe that but for his heavy family responsibilities he would have been prepared to marry her. Yet there is no evidence that the idea ever occurred to him. She apparently kept all his letters and the mention of love or marriage does not exist. From her own confessions, indeed, it is clear that he merely wished to help her with her work. He would have gone to endless trouble to assist any man or woman of talent, and he was far too kind to snub a woman who was obviously infatuated with him.

Madame Avilov was apparently a friend with whom he shared a love of literature, but he never made any effort to seek her out or to arrange a meeting; every first move came from her. His letters to her were on terms of "Yours sincerely". There were, indeed, many such women in Tchehov's life, for as a doctor and a celebrity, women were constantly falling in love with him. But his fine, compassionate nature could not condemn them. He was merely sorry that they should create for themselves such unhappiness. In one of his letters to Madame Avilov, for instance, he wrote, "All my best wishes to you. Above all, be happy; take a less complicated view of life, for it is possibly much simpler in reality."

When August came Tchehov was able to escape from Melihovo for a time, and he took a cheap holiday with his friend Potapenko, of whom he was particularly fond. The two men spent six days on the Psyol. They walked, lazed in the sun, and were extremely happy together. Potapenko was an excellent companion, he was always cheerful, he had a good voice, and he could play the fiddle. The fact that both men were authors was also a great bond.

Then in September Tchehov went to Vienna, and from there to Abbazzia, Fiume, Trieste, Venice, Lemberg and Milan. In Vienna he bought a new inkstand and a jockey-cap with flaps, in Abbazzia it rained heavily from morning till night, and in Venice he contracted a nettlerash! All that remained now, as he jokingly remarked in a letter to his sister, was to go to Genoa, where there was a superb cemetery. To Genoa, therefore, he went, but fortunately the cemetery did not claim him, and he arrived back in Russia in October.

Chapter 19

Meeting with Tolstoy

THE spring of 1895 was a long and dreary one. Deep drifts of snow lay in the fields for weeks and would not melt, the roads were churned up into morasses of mud, and the bitter blustering winds whistled and howled round the house like a myriad devils. Some of the blizzards were truly awful, and the alternate freezing and thawing became horribly depressing. One felt, when the starlings began to sing, that spring was on the way, but the next day every deep rut in the road was frozen again as hard as iron. In the meantime, life and sickness and death went on as before. A message would arrive that a child was ill, a man in mortal agony or a woman in difficult labour, and Tchehov felt obliged to turn out, yet even to reach the village was a hazardous undertaking. Who would be a doctor in such a country?

Visitors from Moscow could not travel, either, in such weather, so to Tchehov in his isolation "the days dragged on like eternity". And then came the inevitable dreary thoughts. Had he been wise to saddle himself with a large estate of 639 acres? It had cost 13,000 roubles, but he had only paid for one-third. There was a mortgage, and also a debt to the bank, both of which would keep him "long years on the chain". This estate, indeed, might prove a heavy burden eventually, for while he could earn, by his writing, four or five thousand roubles a year, all was well, but at the back of his mind was always the growing fear that his health might break down completely. Indeed, at times he wondered, as a doctor, how long he was going to live; there could be little doubt that his illness was affecting his heart. "But what if I depart from you sinners for another world?" he said to Suvorin. "Then the ducal estate with the debts would seem to my parents in their green old age and to my sister such a burden that they would raise a wail to heaven." The very thought of his responsibilities in fact, made him feel old, both in body and spirit. "I have become stupidly indifferent to everything in the world", he confessed . . . "I get up and go to bed feeling as though interest in life had dried up for me."

The behaviour of the peasants, too, was sometimes particularly horrible. One day, for instance, a drunken peasant undressed in view of the house and bathed in the pond. His decrepit old mother beat him with a stick, and the other peasants stood round and giggled. After his bath the peasant walked home barefoot through the snow, followed by his mother. Yet this same old woman had previously been to Tchehov to be treated for bruises after a beating from her son. "And yet", said Tchehov, "we continue to withhold education from the masses. How vile!"

To Suvorin, as usual, Tchehov wrote with complete frankness; he did not attempt to hide his moods. And again Suvorin urged him to think seriously of taking a wife. He had plenty of women friends; it should not be difficult. But to Tchehov there appeared to be many obstacles. Would not a wife be an added responsibility? Besides, he had got into bachelor ways which might be hard to break, and could any author who was obliged to spend many hours in writing, make a woman happy? It would not be possible to earn a living and yet devote oneself to a wife. And experience showed that a marriage could easily disintegrate if a wife felt herself to be neglected. Marriage, surely, meant companionship, and an author was, on the whole, a poor companion. When he was not actually engaged in writing he was inevitably creating and planning his work. Also, what woman would enjoy this isolated existence in the country? Winter in Russia was a terrible season. Most women spent it in Moscow or Petersburg, where there was gaiety and parties, sledge-driving and cosy restaurants.

However, to Suvorin Tchehov was determined to treat the matter lightly. "Very well, I'll get married if you wish it", he wrote. "But my terms are, everything must be just as it was before—that is she must live in Moscow and I in the country and I'll make visits to her. A happiness continued day in day out, from one morning to the next, I cannot endure. When every day I hear the same thing in the same tone, I become furious . . . I promise you to be a splendid husband, but give me a wife who, like the moon, will not appear in my sky every day." And he added, "But I shall not write better for being married".

In the meantime, Marie, determined to bear her share of the burden, tired herself out and was constantly irritable. She tried, in the absence of good labour, to undertake tasks which were obviously beyond her strength. And as Tchehov said, "To advise young ladies to take up farming is much the same as to advise them to be bears, and to bend yokes . . . To live on the land by the labour of one's hands and the sweat of one's brow is only possible . . . if one works oneself like a peasant, without regard to class or sex. There is no making use of slaves nowadays; one must take the scythe and axe oneself . . . Even the smallest success in farming is only gained in Russia at the price of a cruel struggle with Nature, and wishing is not enough for the struggle; you need bodily strength and grit, you want traditions . . ."

Spring came at last, so late and longed-for that it was like a breath of heaven. The green grass, the beautiful trees, the lovely windswept skies, the singing of the nightingales; all were enchanting. The long dreary winter had been worth while. Was not life in the country an exquisite thing? To drive through the forest in the moonlight was a wonderful experience. Tchehov's financial position, too, had improved, for his books were selling well and his stories were now commanding high prices. Indeed, as spring drifted into summer his old gay mood returned. Friends came to stay, the house rang with merry laughter, and life was good again.

Tchehov had now been living at Melihovo for nearly four years. His calves had turned into cows, his copse had grown "at least a yard higher", and the country and its interests had become a part of his life. In Melihovo he had planned many improvements, the most important being the building of a school, at his own expense. He was also assisting in the building of a hospital (badly needed), a fire-station, and a belfry for the church. New roads were being constructed, too, and in the planning of this work Tchehov was taking an active part.

Another event worth recording is that during the summer he paid a visit to Yasnaya Polyana, Tolstoy's home. This estate, which had been in the Tolstoy family for generations, was about 130 miles from Moscow, in the Province of Tula. Set in beautiful surroundings, it was generally the centre of much gaiety and hospitality. Unfortunately a few months previously Tolstoy had lost by death his youngest child, Vanya, aged seven, a very gifted boy in whom his parents had placed great hopes.

Tchehov was received by Tolstoy and his family with much kindness, and was treated as an honoured guest. Tolstoy was, of course, a magnificent personality. He was a brilliant conversationalist, and was keenly interested in Art, education, philosophy, religion and literature. Along the avenue of lime trees and by the river he and Tchehov walked and talked, and although there is no known record of their conversations, it is safe to assume that the older man did most of the talking, as Tchehov never discussed controversial subjects. Indeed, although there were striking similarities in their work, yet as writers they were totally different in their outlook on life. Tolstoy much regretted that Tchehov's work expressed no clear philosophy, and he would have preferred to see him more active and revolutionary on behalf of the peasants. But Tolstoy's attitude to Tchehov's work is best shown in his criticism of Tchehov's exquisite story, *The Darling*, a story which moved Tolstoy to tears. Yet it is clear that he did not understand it, for he believed that Tchehov intended "to mock at the pitiful creature" (the darling). And from this wrong conclusion he jumps to another. "I believe", said Tolstoy, "that while he was writing *The Darling* the author had in his mind, though not in his heart, a vague image of a new woman, of her equality with man; of a woman mentally developed, learned, working independently for the good of society as well as, if not better than a man . . . and in writing *The Darling* he wanted to show what woman ought not to be . . . I am afraid that Tchehov . . . intended to curse, but the god of poetry forbade him and commanded him to bless."

This opinion was, of course, quite a wrong one, for few, if any, of Tchehov's stories have such a purpose, and it is safe to assert that he never for one moment intended to condemn The Darling, nor did he intend to show "what woman ought not to be". Condemnation was not his role.

As for Tchehov's attitude to Tolstoy's work, this was inevitably affected by the difference in their ages, for Tolstoy was thirty-two years older, and was already a celebrated writer when Tchehov was still a boy. There was, surrounding the figure of Tolstoy, a glamour and a brightness which could never wholly be separated from his work. As a matter of fact, Tchehov admired *The Kreutzer Sonata* enormously, both for the gravity of its conception and the beauty of its execution. He considered, too, that it was a lasting contribution to thought. Yet he felt that it had one or two grave defects. As to *War and Peace*, Tchehov had read it with admiration many times, but there were certain passages (principally those parts of the book where Napoleon came on the scene) which seemed to him to be "full of forced explanations and tricks of all sorts".

With regard to Tolstoy's philosophy (a philosophy which had attracted hundreds of disciples), at one time it had moved Tchehov profoundly and had even taken possession of him for some six or seven years, but it had not stood the test of time. "Surely", argued Tchehov, "in the electricity and heat of love for man there is something greater than chastity and abstinence from meat! . . . War is an evil and legal justice is an evil, but from that it does not follow that one ought to wear bark shoes and sleep on the stove with the labourer." Tolstoy's philosophy could not mean progress. "I have peasant blood in my veins", said Tchehov (to Suvorin), "and you won't astonish me with peasant virtues."

When the time came for Tchehov to leave Yasnaya Polyana, the two writers were really sorry to part. It was not, however, to be their last meeting.

Chapter 20

"The Seagull"

HOW quickly the summer had passed! It seemed that no sooner had the corn been gathered in than the leaves began to fall from the trees and autumn was on the way. It was a melancholy season, for it did not come gradually, as in England, and in a blaze of scarlet and gold, but suddenly. The days soon shortened and the nights became long and dark. From the gloomy trees the owls screeched mournfully. And soon, almost without warning, the snow began to fall, tirelessly, incessantly, for days on end. It was beautiful, especially in the moonlight, and yet . . . Tchehov confessed that he marvelled at the fortitude of landowners who spent the winter in the country. He had noticed that unless they were engaged in intellectual work they generally became either gluttons or drunkards. "The monotony of the snowdrifts and the bare trees, the long nights, the moonlight, the deathlike stillness, day and night, the peasant women and the old ladies—all that disposes one to indolence, indifference and an enlarged liver . . ."

It was at this time that Suvorin again urged Tchehov to marry. Would he not seriously consider it? But his reply was the same:—"I am afraid of a wife and domestic routine; the latter would embarrass me and would not accord, I fancy, with my untidiness." But he added, "Still it is better than to drift on the sea of life and beat about in the frail canoe of profligacy."

What could he do, however, to cure these fits of depression? The answer, surely, was to write something into which he could put his whole mind and heart; and Suvorin's suggestion was a play. Tchehov had had an idea for a play in mind for a long time, and although he had declared consistently that he would never again write for the theatre, yet the old hankering remained. Indeed, the characters of his play already existed for him as living entities. He knew their idiosyncrasies, the very clothes they wore, their looks, their gestures; he could see them making love and whispering to each other in the garden, he could see them playing cards in the evening and sitting over the samovar. He could see the sun setting behind the pines, and the evening light glinting across the tranquil lake . . . His play, *The Seagull*, in fact, was coming to birth.

But had he not forgotten the awful birth pangs connected with the creation of a play, the hours of futility and despair, the days when nothing goes right and the play seems banal and meaningless? This could be sheer agony. No, he remembered only too well. But this play shouted insistently to be written. And in the end he was sure something would come of it. His vision was bright enough, and the poetry of the piece was already weaving its spell about him. It was to be a play of middle-class life in the country, with all its beauty and poignancy, its boredom, pettiness, futility and love affairs. It would be a picture of the fascinating tragi-comedy of human life—the struggle between spirit and flesh, the shortness of youth, the pressure of death, the indifference of Nature, the disillusion of old age. But it should show, too, the unquenchable fountain of hope and joy which was a part of every man's heritage.

It was all in his mind. Yet how difficult this play was to write! He had constant palpitations and was sleeping badly. "I am weary of this spinning round," he wrote to Suvorin, "and if monasteries admitted unbelievers, and if it were not the rule there to pray I would become a monk!"

However, the play went steadily ahead, and a theatrical manager, already interested, had promised Tchehov an advance in February if the play was accepted.

The Seagull was finished in November, and sent off to Moscow to be typed. It was not to be produced before the next theatrical season, so many changes might yet be made. When a play was read, after an interval, the inevitable slight inconsistencies and flaws showed up sharply, and that was the time to cut and revise again. For, indeed, on this occasion Tchehov did not intend to fail. He was determined that the public should understand the play. He had written it with loving care, even with ardour, and although he had been obliged to conform to the accepted technique of the stage, nevertheless he could swear with his hand on his heart that he had not falsified life for the sake of dramatic presentation. One could not (as Tolstoy said) invent psychology.

Rehearsals for *The Seagull* were started in September, 1896, and Tchehov went to Petersburg to assist and advise. But the piece was so different from the type of play with which the theatres were familiar, that the actors could not understand it; they were unable, apparently, to portray the subtle characterization or indicate the swift changes of mood which ran through the piece. Indeed, the characters in *The Seagull* were not simply drawn; they were as complex as real human beings. But the characterization was highly important, and the "mood" of the piece had to be felt. Otherwise the play was unintelligible.

As for Tchehov, he almost wept and wrung his hands as he watched the rehearsals. He was appalled by the deplorable acting and the general bewilderment. These men and women who strode about the stage seemed to have no connection with his play; they were utterly wooden, and were apparently incapable of learning their parts. The confusion was awful, and the whole effect was "shadowy, grey, dismal". Was there no one who could understand? Was the play, therefore, so unintelligible? What a fool he had been to write again for the stage! The rehearsals were agonising to watch.

Tchehov was, of course, appealed to for advice. But how could he put these people right? It was not his forte; he had had no experience in such matters, nor, indeed, in dealing with actors. He was far too gentle, tactful and sensitive to criticise others, especially when they were doing their best. Besides, the producer was all powerful, and the players, like most actors of their time, were not highly disciplined, and most of them were touchy and difficult. They wished to please, but could not, apparently, grasp what was to them a new form of dramatic art. The only member of the company who seemed to feel the "tone", in fact, was Madame Kommissarzhevsky. Her acting, at times, was extremely effective and moving.

Tchehov attended only two rehearsals (he had certainly hoped for more), and on both occasions he was profoundly dissatisfied. He thought the scenery inappropriate and the acting hopelessly inadequate. Was this, possibly, always the way with authors? Was he too pernickety? Was he aiming at a standard which was impossible to reach? At any rate, he had never felt so utterly frustrated, and after the last rehearsal he begged for the play to be taken off. But this, at the eleventh hour, was impossible. The actors believed that "everything would be all right on the night". A fatal conclusion! A foolish hope!

The Seagull was produced in Petersburg on the 17th October, 1896, at the Alexandrinsky Theatre. Tchehov sat in the stalls, full of hope (for what else could sustain him?) but inwardly quaking with apprehension. He had warned Suvorin beforehand of his fears, and he was prepared for a fiasco, but what followed was far worse than anything he had anticipated. The actors did not know their parts, they played "woodenly and without conviction", and in the theatre (which was "as hot as hell") there was an atmosphere of boredom and bewilderment. The audience was inattentive, and they talked and laughed consistently during the most pathetic passages. It was clear, too, that Madame Kommissarzhevsky alone understood the play and was carrying the whole piece on her shoulders.

After the second act Tchehov left the stalls and went into one of the actor's dressing-rooms. But matters went from bad to worse, everything seemed to be against the play, and the evening was a complete failure: During one of the intervals Tchehov heard a man in the foyer say, "That's literature and not drama", and his companion replied, "And bad literature at that." A third man asked, "Who is this Tchehov? Where did he spring from?" and another man said, "I can't understand how the administration of the theatre allows such plays to be performed. To put on such plays is an insult."

Tchehov stayed almost until the end, then he fled from the theatre and went out into the damp streets. By the river he paced up and down for a long time; then vexed, bewildered and utterly weary, he went to Romanovs and had supper, alone. Never had he felt so shamed and crushed. He swore to himself that as long as he lived he would never write another play; he had finished with the theatre for ever. The piece was evidently quite unintelligible, even senseless. It was clumsy, and he had created nothing but idiots. Obviously, therefore, his literary powers had come to an end. A bitter thought, indeed!

He arrived back at Suvorin's house, very unhappy and distressed, and in reply to his friend's enquiries confessed that he had been "walking the streets". "If I were to live another seven hundred years I would not give another play to the theatre," he declared. Then, having decided that he could not stay, he sat down to write letters of farewell—to Suvorin, to Michael, and to Marie. He could face no one else at the moment. "I am off to Melihovo," he wrote to Suvorin. "Stop the printing of the plays. I shall never forget yesterday evening . . . I am not going to produce the play in Moscow. I shall never again either write plays or have them acted."

To Michael he wrote, "The play has fallen flat and come down with a crash. There was an oppressive, strained feeling of disgrace and bewilderment in the theatre. The players acted abominably stupidly. The moral of it is one ought not to write plays."

Some hours later Tchehov was on his way to Melihovo; he simply could not face any of his friends. Nor did he relish the task of confessing his failure to his old parents.

They were always so proud of him. For obviously (reasoned Tchehov) it was not the play which had failed but he himself. This was mature work; it could not be compared with *Ivanov*, which had been written hurriedly. The failure of *The Seagull* was a far more serious matter. He had taken such infinite pains over the piece, and before setting pen to paper he had made a most careful study of the technique of the stage.

On his arrival at Melihovo telegrams and messages from Petersburg were waiting for him. From Potapenko came a telegram, sent no doubt with the kindest intentions— "A colossal success", yet one lady—a complete stranger— wrote to express her sympathy in such mournful terms that her letter could only have been appropriate had he lost a beloved member of his family. From Suvorin came a letter which blamed Tchehov for his flight from Petersburg, called him "womanish" and said that he had "left in a funk". This letter certainly stung Tchehov a little—as Suvorin probably intended—but actually he was too tired and depressed to care greatly what anyone said. He knew that under the circumstances he could not possibly have behaved otherwise.

When the press notices arrived, Tchehov lived the whole ghastly nightmare over again. The critics were very prejudiced and hostile, and suggested the most wildly impossible reasons for the failure of the play. They also declared that *The Seagull* was "lacking in talent, unintelligible, even nonsensical". They announced pompously that he was "no playwright, but was vainly trying to be one". One newspaper published a mass of correspondence which suggested that Tchehov's literary rivals had organised a scandal against him in the theatre, and another critic asked, "What wrong has Tchehov done to his friends?" Tchehov read them all, and marvelled at the insincerity, stupidity and malice of Russian critics. He felt as though he had stumbled into a foul-smelling pond.

By the same post, too, came many letters—both signed and anonymous—praising the play and abusing the critics. Tchehov was grateful for these, yet there was little consolation in them, for obviously if kind-hearted people felt that it was necessary to comfort him, then surely he was in a bad way, and his work was worthless.

However, *The Seagull* was performed again on two occasions, and was very successful. As Suvorin had prophesied, the actors had lost their nervousness, they had learnt their parts and now understood the play. A few days later Tchehov agreed to the publishing of a collected volume of his plays, and although when the proofs arrived he could hardly bear to read them, yet he had at last come to look on *The Seagull* without loathing.

Before the end of the year, too, news arrived from Petersburg that the play was in great demand. It seemed that that disastrous first night had proved to be an excellent advertisement. *The Seagull* had raised such a storm of controversy that its future was assured.

But the writing of the play, the heartrending rehearsals, and the bitter disappointment of that first night had left their mark. The fun had gone out of life, and it seemed to Tchehov that "the daily round, the common task" were barely worthwhile. At this time, too, he received an urgent call from his old friend Lika, asking him to meet her in Moscow on "very important business". What this business was is not known. It is only clear the Tchehov returned to Melihovo worried and dispirited. He had always taken the troubles of his friends very much to heart.

His mood at this time, in fact, is clearly shown in his letter to a writer friend, a man to whom he could speak freely:—"We have no politics, no social life, nor even a street life. Our town existence is poor, monotonous, oppressive and uninteresting. You will say that we are writers and that in itself makes our life a rich one. Are you sure? We are embedded in our profession up to our ears; it has gradually isolated us from the outside world and as a result we have little time, little money, few books, we read little and reluctantly, we hear little, we travel little . . . Every year, the same thing, the same thing, and all our talk about

literature is usually reduced to discussing who writes better
and who worse . . ."

Such was Tchehov's mood at this time. But it did
not last. It was merely one of the black periods which are
inevitable in the life of an artist. Tchehov was not robust,
and he would not have been the great artist he was without
this intensity of feeling. How quickly, too, his mood could
change! And when visitors arrived he joked and laughed as
if he had not a care in the world. For was it not one's duty
to hide one's feelings? Was it not bad enough to feel depressed oneself without casting a gloom over others?
Besides, his young admirers—friends of Marie's—who were
continually round the house, expected to be amused, and
laughter was such an excellent medicine. When one young
girl, therefore, pointed out that Tchehov's pigeons—some of
which were white and some coffee-coloured—displayed
similar markings to his cat, he suggested that the pigeons
had probably originated from a crossing of the cat and the
ordinary grey pigeons. The idea was ludicrous, of course,
yet apparently the naive and gullible young girl believed
the story and repeated it in Moscow literary circles!

Chapter 21

Serious illness

IN January, 1897, a census was taken in Russia, and Tchehov was again asked for his assistance. He had had experience of this work in Sahalin, and was therefore asked to train the other enumerators. He also took an active part in the actual work, although he was far from well and suffered from continual fever and weakness. The Government had served out to the enumerators "detestable inkpots, detestable clumsy badges like the labels of a brewery, and portfolios into which the census forms would not fit". It was, Tchehov declared, "a disgrace". But quite apart from these inconveniences the work was extremely tiring. From early morning till late at night he had to go from hut to hut, taking particulars from the occupants. And the doorways were so low that one was continually knocking one's head. As a doctor he was familiar with the peasants' huts, with their fleas, squalor and unkempt children, but in his present state of health the whole task was unpleasant.

Apart from visiting the huts he had to give lectures, and to count and write until his fingers ached. The enumerators worked splendidly, but the Government officials appointed by the Zemstvo were worse than useless. They did nothing, understood little, and at the most difficult periods pretended to be ill. It was unpleasant to be obliged to fraternise with them; and Tchehov was profoundly thankful when his task was done.

He was not, however, to be left in peace, for a few days later a deputation of peasants arrived with a request that he would build another school. There was a serious dearth of peasant schools in the neighbourhood, and there was apparently no one else to turn to, so although he felt quite incapable of undertaking any further public work he finally agreed to do what they asked.

The peasants had collected three hundred roubles towards the cost of the school, but unfortunately three thousand roubles would be needed. So again Tchehov drove round the countryside, appealing for subscriptions—a tiring and thankless task—and finally, as he did not succeed in raising the necessary sum, he made good the deficiency himself. Then came the building of the school, with all its plans and supervision. By the time he had interviewed contractors, builders and architects, it was obvious to his family and friends that he had seriously overtaxed his strength. But he refused to rest until every detail of the new school was settled. At the end of March, however, his endurance had reached breaking-point, and while dining with Suvorin at "The Hermitage" in Moscow, he had a serious haemorrhage from the lungs. He was driven to Suvorin's house, where he was put to bed, and there he remained for two days. But in the early hours of the morning of March 24th he insisted upon returning to his hotel, pleading that he had a mass of correspondence to deal with and many people to see. Suvorin did his utmost to persuade the sick man not to leave, but Tchehov was quite adamant and as a result he had a serious relapse two days later. This could not be ignored, and he was moved to the University Clinic in Moscow. There he was forced to obey orders; he was not allowed to talk, to move or to sit up.

When visitors were allowed, Suvorin came to see him, and was delighted to find him laughing and joking in the most light-hearted way. But when the publisher happened casually to mention that he had watched the breaking up of the ice on the Moscow river, Tchehov's face changed and he asked anxiously, "Has the thaw started?" It was an unfortunate remark, as Suvorin immediately realised, for he remembered how Tchehov, in speaking of peasant patients some days before, had said, "When they are ill with tuberculosis they always say 'Nothing can be done; I shall go as soon as the spring waters begin to flow'."

In the meantime, Tchehov's doctors were seeking to discover the extent of the damage, and eventually they diagnosed an injury at the apex of the lungs. It was a serious matter, and he was solemnly warned that he must change his mode of life. Smilingly he promised to consider what he could do. Had he not in the past made many resolutions to take life more easily? But work was continually thrust upon him; it seemed to be his fate. A whole organisation rested upon his shoulders and he could not possibly fail his family. Also, as with most geniuses, his immense creative energy gave him no rest.

Friends were very kind at this time, and gifts and messages arrived almost hourly. As usual, there were many visitors, one of whom was Tolstoy, who stayed for an hour. For no one dared to hint to this influential genius that the invalid was getting overtired. Indeed, some hours after Tolstoy's departure Tchehov was very ill again and had another attack of haemorrhage.

Finally Tchehov's medical advisers warned him that they could not answer for the consequences unless he lived a very quiet life and resided permanently in the country. He could continue to live at Melihovo, which was dry and healthy, but they suggested that the house should be made warmer and more comfortable. They also strongly advised Tchehov to give up his medical work. Someone else must be found who could bear the burden. Tchehov therefore announced through Marie that he could no longer work in the village as a doctor. And in the meantime, what of himself? He realised that his advisers were right, and yet . . . to live permanently in the country, without an occasional visit to Moscow, was a prospect he could not face. Life in the country brought its joys, but it entailed "constant bothers with peasants, with animals, with things of all kinds". It was, in fact (Tchehov declared) "as easy to guard from burns in hell as from the troubles and bothers of a village". Farming was an excellent thing for a strong, healthy yeoman, but for an author-doctor who possessed a sensitive social conscience, and was suffering from tuber-

culosis, farming and village life were quite unsuitable. He
had bought the place for his health's sake, for the sake of
his family and because he loved the country, but he had
not foreseen the many serious drawbacks. The truth was
that he had not the moral courage to refuse help when
demanded. Besides, these humble people—many of whom
were very worthy (he had championed their cause for
years)—relied on him and trusted him. He was proud to
have been of use to them

By April 10th Tchehov was home again, and up and
about. He was still weak, but he could manage a little
gardening, and he succeeded in pruning one rose tree each
day. The supervision of the farm, however, was beyond
his strength, and he was obliged to put this into other hands.
This lack of occupation made life rather dreary, yet in
every other way he insisted that he was feeling "splendid".
He spent the summer quietly in Melihovo, as he was still
supervising the building of the school at Novosiolki, a task
which occupied much of his spare time. But early in July
the school was finished; he attended the opening ceremony,
and was presented with an ikon and an inscription from the
peasants. He also received at about this time a medal in
recognition of his work on the census.

But when August came he was strongly advised by
his doctors to go abroad again, to the South. In the first
week of September, therefore, he left Russia for Biarritz,
and from there, on the advice of friends, he went on to Nice,
where he was fortunate in finding a Russian pension in the
Rue Gounod which suited him admirably. He was given
a large, comfortable south room, a dressing-room, and a
bed "fit only for Cleopatra". Tchehov paid 11 francs a
day, and the food, prepared by a Russian cook, was excellent. The sea was "caressing and tender", the sun shone,
and he was well enough to walk on the promenade and to
gamble a little, though this tired him.

Many Russians were living in Nice at this time, and
with these people Tchehov soon became acquainted.
Maxim Kovalevsky, who owned a villa in Beaulieu, was

perhaps the most interesting. He was a tall, stout, vivacious man, who loved good food, good company and good conversation. He was the best tonic and the best company in the world, and when Tchehov and other Russian friends used to dine with him they would spend the evening in peals of laughter. Tchehov became very attached to Kovalevsky.

Other Russians in Nice at that time with whom Tchehov became friendly were Prince Sumbatov, V. M. Sobolesky, V. I. Nemirovitch-Dantchenko (the dramatist) —who was to play such an important part in Tchehov's later life—and Tchehov's very old friend, Potapenko. In this company the days passed merrily, and life in Nice was so delightful that on the advice of his doctor Tchehov decided to spend the winter there. But in order to do so work was imperative. During the last few months he had written scarcely a line, and what was far more serious, he had felt little desire to write. Occasionally he would resolutely sit down and write a short story, but to write in a hotel room, at an unfamiliar table, and in lovely weather when he longed only to be outdoors, was very difficult. A strange lethargy, too, seemed to have settled upon him, and although he suspected that the state of his health was to blame, yet he was ashamed of his idleness. "Rest", said the doctors, "while you can; it is essential to rest." But the Pension Russe was full of idle people, Russian ladies who were supposed to be "taking the cure". They spent their days in boredom and uselessness, and Tchehov dreaded to think that he might grow like them.

In the meantime, the Dreyfus affair was causing a great sensation and was being widely discussed. Tchehov was studying the case from the shorthand notes, and as a result he was firmly convinced of the innocence of both Zola and Dreyfus. The trial, also, seemed to him to be monstrously unfair, and a series of "grave mistakes in the procedure had been revealed"; The whole thing, in fact, was "a fundamental violation of justice". At the trial Dreyfus had behaved as a well disciplined and decent

officer, but people present at the trial—chiefly journalists—
had shouted at him, "Shut up, Judas".

The *Novoye Vremya*, however, was apparently con-
ducting a campaign against Zola which seemed to Tchehov
to be monstrously unfair. Tchehov stoutly defended Zola
to Suvorin, and insisted that it was not the duty of writers
to accuse or persecute. "There are plenty of accusers,
prosecutors and gendarmes without them", he said. But
what angered Tchehov most was the fact that the *Novoye
Vremya* was publishing Zola's novel, gratis, and at the same
time, in another part of the paper, abusing him. Also,
Tchehov felt that it was a gross breach of literary etiquette
to abuse Zola while he was still on trial, as the *Novoye Vremya*
had done. Such conduct was indefensible.

A great deal of correspondence passed between
Tchehov and Suvorin on this subject, and although Suvorin
endeavoured to justify himself and his newspaper, Tchehov
insisted that the *Novoye Vremya* had taken up an entirely
wrong and unjust attitude. As friends they could afford to
be frank, but when each man had said his say, both were
extremely angry. It was Tchehov, however, who was the
more indignant of the two, as he considered that Suvorin's
newspaper had behaved "simply abominably" over the
case. He was devoted to Suvorin and they had known
each other now for many years, but on this matter they
could not see eye to eye. And so ended a great friendship.
They were to meet later, but never on the same friendly
terms.

Meanwhile, Tchehov remained in Nice, where life
was very pleasant and carefree, and where he had made
for himself a large circle of friends. It was only when
Easter drew near that he became homesick again for his
native land. To celebrate Easter in strange surroundings
seemed wrong, and he could not reconcile himself to the
thought. How well he remembered other Easters in
Moscow! He and his family and friends had always attended
the midnight services, going from one church to another,
and then returned home to the traditional Easter breakfast.

Such a spread! And there had been so much hand-shaking, and kissing and giving of presents. Yes, suddenly he longed to be back in Russia—his dear native land. He longed to see Melihovo again and his horses and dogs. He could picture his old mother, as she had sat so often, bending over the lamp with her needlework. How delightful it would be to see them all again, to watch Marie feeding the geese, driving the cows from the pasture, smiling up at him as she swung lazily in the garden! What would he not give to smell the rain-wet lilacs again, to see the wind sweep over the golden rye, to watch the moon rise over the lake, and see the evening star, shining like a great diamond, in the dark sky? What would he not give to hear the night-ingales again, singing their hearts out?

But Easter passed, and as the weather was still cold he was advised by his doctors to remain in Nice for the time being. He did not, therefore, return to Russia until May. He had been away eight months.

It was delightful to be back in Melihovo, and to be greeted by an exquisite Spring. But life in the country quickly resumed its old character. Visitors to the house became as importunate as ever, and again they encroached upon his time, disturbed him in his work and followed him everywhere. He bore with them patiently, but they no longer amused him. And, indeed, he had changed since his return from Nice. He could still make the house-party rock with laughter, but his laughter came less often and he was more thoughtful. Life, in fact, seemed to be racing on ...

The summer passed uneventfully, and in September, on the advice of his doctors, Tchehov went to Yalta. Here his health improved so much that he decided to settle there and build a house. He disliked hotels, and was tired of continual wandering. He would be obliged, of course, to sell Melihovo, but the estate needed constant supervision, and his father was old and ill, and not likely to live long. After his death the last link with Melihovo would be gone, as Tchehov's mother would not care to live alone in the country during the winter. Besides, Yalta was a pleasant spot, and the climate was particularly suited to his complaint. It was many miles from Moscow, and his happy circle of friends, but he was convinced that the doctors were right. He might possibly live the full span of life if he made some effort to safeguard his health.

Chapter 22

The Moscow Art Theatre Company

TCHEHOV'S connection with play-writing had ceased, and he had vowed, time and time again, that he had finished with the theatre; past experiences had been too painful. The public did not understand his work, actors consistently bungled it, and producers had frankly confessed themselves bewildered by his plays.

The theatre, in fact, was a part of his life which must be buried, once and for all. He did not intend to slave over the creation of a play, attend agonising rehearsals, battle with puzzled producers, and then be mortified by a ghastly failure. Never again!

But his passionate interest in the theatre was not dead; the flames had died down, perhaps, but the embers were ready to be fanned into life. And by an odd coincidence this is exactly what happened. For in Nice he had met that brilliant man, Vladimir Ivanovitch Nemirovitch-Dantchenko; it was a meeting which was to produce remarkable results. Nemirovitch was a dramatist and a teacher of dramatic art. He was regarded, in fact, as one of the best of the younger playwrights, and he had already been awarded half the Griboyedov prize for one of his plays, the other half having been given to Tchehov. Nemirovitch, however, had declined his share of the prize in favour of Tchehov, whose greater gifts he freely acknowledged, and whose work he admired immensely.

Nemirovitch had just formed, in partnership with Constantin Stanislavsky (an extremely talented actor who was passionately devoted to the theatre) the Moscow Art Theatre Company. They had gathered together a group of highly talented and enthusiastic actors, and their aim was to produce plays by contemporary authors which were representative of life in Russia. They intended at the same time to rejuvenate the art of the theatre, and they were particularly anxious to revive *The Seagull*.

Stanislavsky, the son of a wealthy Russian merchant, and the grandson of a French actress, was a most interesting man. Acting was in his blood, and the stage was his passion, his hobby, his love, his life; it was a passion that was shared by his wife, family and friends. Business, in comparison, meant nothing to him; it was the theatre which occupied all his waking thoughts.

Never were two men so well met as Stanislavsky and Nemirovitch, for both had the same aims, and both were experienced actors. When the two men decided to form their company they were so excited that they talked almost unceasingly from two o'clock in the afternoon until eight o'clock the following morning. Both men had been dreaming of this project for years.

Stanislavsky was a man of great determination, and Nemirovitch was the sort of director of whom one might dream; he had had a wide literary education, he possessed great administrative ability, and he had the most exquisite taste and judgment. He begged Tchehov now, at the beginning of their venture, to allow him to produce *The Seagull*. Nemirovitch was convinced that it had failed in Petersburg merely because it had been wrongly produced, but he was certain that he could produce it successfully.

Tchehov was extremely interested in this new venture, and was much impressed by the two directors. He also agreed that the theatre urgently needed new methods and new talent; the old conventions had become banal, dull, outworn. Nemirovitch, too, was apparently one of the few men who understood his plays. On the other hand, Tchehov remembered only too well that miserable first night years ago when *The Seagull* was presented. He had no desire to repeat the experience. It was many months, in fact, before Tchehov could bring himself to consider this new proposal, but finally he gave way, and it was arranged that

the Company should start work on *The Seagull*. Nemirovitch was in ecstasies, and Stanislavsky—who had the
highest opinion of his co-director's judgment but was
uncertain as to the merits of Tchehov's plays—held his
tongue and waited.

In the meantime, the Company was being strictly
trained, and every member was made to realise that in the
sacred cause of Art discipline was essential.   Their chief
maxims were "All disobedience to the creative life of the
theatre is a crime" and "Unpunctuality, laziness, caprice,
hysterics, bad character, ignorance of the role, the necessity
of repeating anything twice, are all equally harmful to our
enterprise and must be rooted out."   Their aim was to
create one of the finest theatres in the world, but they
realised that they had much to learn.   They knew, too,
that compared with its European rivals, the Russian theatre
was a very young institution.   This talented Company were
a merry crowd, and although they quarrelled occasionally
(as was inevitable), and it was not unusual to find an
actress weeping bitterly when rehearsals proved too difficult
and exhausting, yet on the whole they worked well together.
It was, indeed, essential for them to succeed, as the popular
press were inclined to sneer at their efforts, as mediocre
amateurs who were obliged to bolster themselves up with
rich costumes and scenery.   The new venture was ridiculed
as merely the hobby of a merchant and his dilettante
friends.   Stanislavsky and Nemirovitch were determined,
therefore, that every production should be as perfect as
human hands and brains could make it; nothing must be
overlooked; nothing must be false.   They had set themselves
the highest possible standard, and by all that was holy it
should be reached.

Tchehov had the utmost faith in the new Company
and prophesied a great future for it.   "Once cultured people
are at its head and not theatrical mountebanks, the theatre
cannot but be successful", he said.   But the first reading of
the play—for which he went specially to Moscow—did not
go well.   Stanislavsky did not understand the piece, nor

could he appreciate the beauty and poetry of this original play. The actors and actresses appeared to be equally bewildered; they could make little of it. There was still, however, the author; surely he could explain what was wanted! But when they asked Tchehov's advice he seemed ill at ease, and answered either humorously or irrelevantly. His delightful personality charmed them all, but apparently he had little talent for teaching or directing; he seemed to dislike any discussion of his work, and became agitated and embarrassed.

The plot, for instance, seemed to be as haphazard as life itself. The dialogue, too, appeared to be on the level of ordinary speech, and the characters frequently spoke at cross purposes; they were not interested in each other; they did not answer each other or show any sympathy. One man spoke of literature, another raved of love, one rambled on about the past, another was entirely engrossed in his health, and a fifth was obviously thinking only of the next meal. This was as realistic as life itself, but on the stage it had to be woven into a coherent whole, which meant that every actor had to get into the exact mood of the character he was representing; it was not merely a question of characterisation. The play, in fact, contained no simple characters; these people were all drawn in the round; they had their faults, their idiosyncrasies, and their very real virtues; they had their moments of nobility, even, and their deplorable lapses into folly. No actor could say, therefore, "Is this man a fool or a rogue?", or, "Is he a villain or a hero?". To Tchehov life was not as simple as that, and human nature was far more complex.

Tchehov, for his part, returned from that rehearsal delighted with the prospects of the new venture. "The intelligent and fine tone of the Company," their youth, their enthusiasm and their real ability to work had greatly impressed him. They had not yet had time to acquire a finished technique, but they were excellent material for a new technique, such as he now realised his plays demanded.

And amongst this company there was one fascinating

actress, above all, who had left a most vivid memory; this was the auburn-haired Hungarian, Olga Leonardovna Knipper. From his seat in the back of the stalls Tchehov had watched her with increasing admiration. Her voice, her sincerity, and the grace and beauty of her had moved him deeply.

Tchehov paid a further visit to Moscow in October in order to discuss with Stanislavsky and Nemirovitch the production of *The Seagull*, and during this visit he attended a rehearsal at The Hermitage Theatre of *Tsar Fyodor*, which the Moscow Art Theatre Company were presenting before the production of *The Seagull*. He was charmed with the whole performance, and it seemed to him that there was real art on the stage. But "best of all", he said, "was Irene" (Olga Knipper). "If I remained in Moscow I should fall in love with that Irene."

It was impossible, however, to remain in Moscow. For his health's sake he was obliged to return almost at once to Yalta, and from there, by correspondence, he was kept informed of the progress of events. How eagerly, now, he looked for news! For already these actors and directors had become his near and dear friends.

The Moscow Art Theatre Company, in their determination to revitalise the art of the theatre, intended to change all the old, out-worn conventions—the star system (which spoilt the ensemble), the florid and inartistic scenery, the orchestra (with its absurd polka and castanets), and the exaggerated gestures, bathos and declamation of conventional acting. The bright wings of red which were used in front of the footlights were abolished, the red curtain, painted with golden tassels and drapery, was declared hideous, and in its place was substituted a graceful cloth curtain of a subdued colour which would not clash with the scenic effects on the stage. And finally, the orchestra was entirely dispensed with, for Stanislavsky decided that its music did not add to the atmosphere they wished to create.

But the new company were not able to make all these drastic changes in a few weeks. They had first to deal with many difficulties, most of which would have permanently discouraged all but the most enthusiastic artists. In the first place, they could not find a suitable theatre. The Hermitage, therefore, was rented as a temporary substitute, but this theatre was in a deplorable condition. It was ill-constructed, dirty, dusty, unheated, and permeated with the smell of beer and some sort of acid, as a result of the summer letting of the theatre. Acrobats, clowns, panto-mimists and trained animals had left unpleasant evidence of their ill manners everywhere, and there were posters and advertisements on the walls. In addition, none of the chimneys was fit for use—so the theatre could not be heated—and the electric lighting plant was out of order.

All this had to be put right, and it was as difficult as turning a stable into a temple (as Stanislavsky remarked). He and Nemirovitch, however, soon arranged for sub-stantial alterations and repairs, but they were anxious to lose no time in producing their first play (*Tsar Fyodor*) as the funds of the company were getting very low. The rehearsals, therefore, could not be postponed, and while workmen hammered night and day, the distracted actors strode up and down, trying to make themselves heard above the din. They were wrapped in their greatcoats because of the intense cold, and many of the rehearsals also had to take place in semi-darkness until the electric lighting plant was repaired.

Other difficulties arose as the rehearsals proceeded, but these were met with a courage and resourcefulness which was worthy of the highest praise; the actors resolutely refused to be discouraged.

It was clear that the Company would be judged by their first production (*Tsar Fyodor*), and if it was not suc-cessful their new venture was doomed. Stanislavsky and Nemirovitch, therefore, made sketches in the museums and art galleries of every costume and effect which had a bearing on the play, they scoured the city for old engravings, and visited antique shops, palaces, monasteries, etc. in search of old armour, monastic and ecclesiastical robes, old embroidery and ancient Russian head-dresses. Stanislavsky even visited some of the medieval cities of Russia in search of materials and effects, as he was determined that every detail of the production should be perfect.

The first performance of *Tsar Fyodor* took place on October 14th, 1898, and was a brilliant success. The critics gave excellent notices, and the future of the Company seemed assured. Unfortunately Tchehov was not well enough to be present at that first night, but he received the good news by telegram. He was delighted, and only one small fact marred his pleasure; Olga Knipper had not received from the critics the notice and praise he had hoped for. "Why don't they speak of Olga Knipper?" he demanded of Nemirovitch.

Chapter 23

Revival of "The Seagull"

WHEN the rehearsals for *The Seagull* began in earnest, Stanislavsky was puzzled and bewildered by his task; he could make no headway. He could not, in fact, understand why Nemirovitch was so enraptured with the play, and it was Stanislavsky's belief that "nothing would come of it" and that it was totally unsuited to the theatre. However, he was willing to bow to Nemirovitch in such matters, and he resolutely set himself to bring the play to life. This, he soon realised, could not be achieved until the spiritual reality of the piece was felt by every member of the cast, and until he had created on the stage the exact "mood" or atmosphere. Towards this end the Company worked unceasingly. But it was only after many rehearsals and many long and anxious discussions that *The Seagull* took living shape.

The play was really produced under the most difficult conditions, and at great risk, as the Company needed money urgently; it was therefore essential to get the piece on as soon as possible. Unfortunately, when the rehearsals were almost at an end, bad news came from Yalta; Tchehov was ill again. This information threw the whole company into a panic, for they felt that if the play was a failure Tchehov would never weather the blow. According to their high standards the production was far from perfect, yet they could not afford to wait any longer.

As the opening night drew near, the actors lived and worked in a fever of apprehension, and Tchehov's sister was so convinced that the play would be a failure that on the eve of the first performance she wept and implored Stanislavsky to postpone the production. But this, at the eleventh hour, was quite impossible. There were only six hundred roubles in the box office, and the Company could not face a financial loss.

The Seagull was presented to a small but chosen audience on December 17th, 1898, and although the actors were extremely nervous they acted magnificently. Every member of the Company realised that this production must not fail.

As the curtain fell after the first act there was an awful silence, and Olga Knipper, unable to stand the strain, fainted on the stage. In despair the actors began to move towards their dressing-rooms, but suddenly there was a roar and thunder of applause from the auditorium; the audience had apparently been almost spellbound for a few moments and could not express its feelings. The curtain rose and fell, and rose again and again, as the applause continued. Then followed congratulations and embraces as on Easter night. One actor went into hysterics, and others leapt and danced about in their joy. It was a wonderful evening. The audience had apparently taken *The Seagull* to their hearts, and the Art Theatre Company was established, once for all. They had succeeded in presenting, in all its richness, subtlety and fineness, the work of this great but unorthodox artist. Nemirovitch had been right.

A joyous telegram was despatched to Tchehov, and he, from his sickbed, sent them his grateful thanks and congratulations. It had been a bitter disappointment that he had not been able to be present, but he assured them that he would come later. Indeed, his whole being yearned for Moscow, and for those charming talented people whose interests he had so deeply at heart.

As for the critics, Prince Urusov wrote:—"Moscow has positively fallen in love with *The Seagull*," and he declared that "at moments it seemed that life itself was speaking from the stage". Those critics who had previously damned the play now also lost no time in praising it fulsomely; they could not judge for themselves, but were willing to follow like foolish sheep.

It was many weeks before Tchehov's convalescence was complete, and by that time the theatre season in Moscow had ended; the Company had scattered, and the theatre was let for the summer. But Tchehov begged to be allowed to see just one performance of his play. Could it not be arranged? Stanislavsky, however, was obliged to point out that all their belongings had been taken away and stored in a small barn, so in order to show a single performance they would have to hire a theatre, and stage hands to unpack the scenery, properties, costumes, wigs, etc., etc. It would be necessary to collect the actors, rehearse them, and instal the lighting system. It seemed an impossible task.

Nevertheless, the kind-hearted and resourceful Stanislavsky was so anxious to please the author that he hired the Nikitsky theatre and gave a special performance. A few friends also attended, and Tchehov was delighted with the play. After every act he ran on to the stage and went into each dressing-room to talk to the actors. "It was wonderful, wonderful!" he said. He did not, however, agree that the author Trigorin (played by Stanislavsky) should have been presented as a dandy; he should have been carelessly dressed. Authors were rarely immaculate.

And now, too, Tchehov was able to renew his acquaintance with Olga Knipper, the actress he had so much admired on his previous visit. He also invited her to Melihovo, and in May she spent three days with himself and his family.

Olga was completely fascinated by the Tchehovs and their charming miniature estate, and during this short holiday she and Tchehov became great friends.

So the spring passed and summer came. Tchehov stayed on at Melihovo, and Olga was on holiday in the Caucasus, but she had promised to write to him and they had planned to meet in Yalta at the end of the summer if it could be arranged. She had not written, however. "What does this mean?" wrote Tchehov. "Where are you? You so persistently send me no news of yourself that we are lost in conjecture and are beginning to think that you

have forgotten us and have got married in the Caucasus . . .
The author is forgotten. Oh, how awful, how treacherous
that is, how cruel!"

But Olga was not married, nor had she forgotten the
author. She wrote in reply and suggested that they might
meet in July and travel together to Batum and Yalta.
Tchehov thought the suggestion an "enchanting" one. "I
will come," he said . . . "but only on the condition . . . that
you will not turn my head."

So plans were made, and finally they met on the
steamer at Novorossiisk on the 18th of July, and travelled
together to Yalta. There Olga stayed with some friends,
while Tchehov stayed at the Hotel Marino on the sea front.
But they met almost daily and spent many happy hours
together. There was so much to discuss, for both were
passionately devoted to the theatre, and Olga was a great
admirer of his work.

Tchehov had now bought a piece of land at Yalta,
and his house was in process of being built. Turks and
Tartars had dug the ground and laid the foundations, and
every day he went to watch the work. It was fascinating to
see the house grow, and he was secretly hoping that Olga,
too, might eventually share it with him, for never before
had he been so deeply attracted to any woman. It was not
her beauty alone which fascinated him, but her warmth and
gaiety, her intelligence and her charming personality.
Indeed, when it was time for Olga to return to her work
he could not bear to part with her and decided to accompany
her to Moscow. In August, therefore, they started on their
long journey, driving first over the Ai-Petri mountain and
through the beautiful Kokkoz valley.

In Moscow the time was spent in seeing old friends
and watching rehearsals, but Tchehov soon realised that
the heat and dust of Moscow were adversely affecting his
health, so he stayed for only three weeks. On his return to
Yalta the new house was finished. Built of white stone, in
a modern style, and beautifully proportioned, it was surely
the most original house in Yalta. Through its many win-

dows the bright sunlight streamed all day. There was a wide, glass-roofed verandah on the ground floor, and an open terrace above. There was also a "watch-tower", from which one could get a very fine view of sea and mountains.

The house stood in its own garden and orchard, and on the opposite side of the road was an old disused cemetery surrounded by a low wall. No one ever came with flowers to this deserted spot, and the graves had sunk into the long grass. But Tchehov was not depressed by the cemetery; it was all so green and peaceful.

Guarded by the faithful "Mustapha" (the Turkish caretaker) Tchehov now installed himself, and with great enthusiasm began to design the garden. He planted roses, bulbs of every description, and shrubs, thorns and small trees. Indeed, when his mother and sister arrived they were enraptured with the place. (His father was dead and Melihovo had now been sold.)

Yet what was different about Anton? His mother was puzzled, for surely he was more thoughtful and absent-minded than he had ever been! Was it, thought Marie, the charming Olga who was responsible? She could not remember her bachelor brother behaving in quite this way before. It is true, they were all continually urging him to marry. Michael had made it very plain some months ago. But Tchehov had replied, "As for me marrying, on which you insist, well how shall I put it? It is only interesting to marry for love; but to marry a girl just because she is sympathetic is like buying an unnecessary article in the market merely because it is nice. In family life the most important thing is love, sexual attraction, one flesh; all the rest is dreary and cannot be reckoned upon, however cleverly we make our calculations. So the point is not in the girl's being nice but in her being loved; putting it off, as you see, counts for little . . ."

It was not possible for Tchehov, in fact, to open his heart unreservedly to anyone. But the truth was that in his new home his thoughts turned constantly in the direction of Moscow. He and Olga could not meet again until the spring; it seemed an eternity. Ah, she was already the image round which all his hopes and desires were centred. "Dear, marvellous actress", he wrote . . . "I bow down very low to you, so low that my forehead touches the bottom of my well, which is forty feet deep now. I have grown used to being with you, and now I cannot reconcile myself to the thought that I shall not see you again until the spring . . ."

Meanwhile, in Yalta there were "insufferable" crowds of visitors, all day and every day. "I rage and rage", he wrote to Olga, "and envy the very rat that lives under the floor of your theatre."

Chapter 24

"Uncle Vanya"
and "The Three Sisters"

THE Moscow Art Theatre continued to flourish, and on the 26th October, 1899, they produced *Uncle Vanya* (adapted from *The Wood Demon*), which was given a brilliant reception. Telegrams of congratulation were immediately despatched to Tchehov, and they began to arrive on the night of the 27th, so were sent on by telephone. Each time the telephone rang he woke up to take the message. But could any author resent such interruptions to his sleep? It was, as he remarked to Olga, the first time that his own fame had kept him awake.

His fortieth birthday, too, was made the occasion for many kind messages and congratulations, and he was elected a Member of the Academy of Literature. Yet all this kindness merely served to remind him of the distance between himself and Moscow, where his real interests lay. He felt that although Yalta was probably curing him of tuberculosis, yet it was making him feel ten years older. The winter seemed interminable.

In the meantime, Stanislavsky and Nemirovitch were constantly but tactfully reminding Tchehov that a new play from him would be a godsend; it would make all the difference to their finances and reputation. *Uncle Vanya* had been very successful, but they were so anxious to produce a new play.

Tchehov read their letters with a sigh, but what they asked was impossible. He was engaged in the heavy task of editing the collected edition of all his works, many of which had appeared in various periodicals over a period of nearly twenty years. He had sold the copyright of his works to Marx, the publisher, for the sum of 75,000 roubles, and the stories, all selected by himself, were to be published in a ten volume edition. This meant that Marx had the sole right to publish his works in book form, but Tchehov still retained the right to publish his stories in magazines and periodicals in the usual way. He had also reserved for himself the income from his plays.

This arrangement had several advantages; it meant that his books would be published creditably, that he would be spared the bother of dealing with printers and booksellers, and that he could work quietly without fear of the future. The income would not be a large one, but it would be constant.

The correcting of the proofs, too, was a heavy task, but it could not be postponed, nor could it be delegated. All this he explained to Nemirovitch, and to assure him that he was still vitally interested in the theatre he said, "Oh, don't get tired. Don't cool off." (Nemirovitch had complained of the worry of theatrical details.) "The Art Theatre will provide the best of the history, when it is written, of the modern Russian theatre . . . It is the only theatre I love."

But Nemirovitch and Stanislavsky were not satisfied, and they decided to go to Yalta to see Tchehov himself, in order to persuade him to write a new play. They decided, in fact, to take the whole Company on tour to Sevastopol, and to play *The Seagull*, *Uncle Vanya*, Hauptmann's *Lonely Lives* and Ibsen's *Hedda Gabler*. Tchehov had never seen a real production by the Company, and they were anxious to show him how greatly their work had improved. It would be their first tour, and a complicated undertaking, as not only would they take the actors, and their wives, children and nurses, but also the stage hands, property men, costumiers, wigmakers and several carloads of property and scenery. Many admirers of Tchehov's work, amongst whom was a well-known critic, were also anxious to accompany them. It would be a merry party.

This was the most wonderful news for Tchehov, and with renewed energy he turned his attention to the garden, and made innumerable alterations and improvements. Olga had promised to stay with him and his family for Holy Week, and everything must be perfect. Not since last autumn had he worked with such enthusiasm.

Olga, more lovely and bewitching than ever, arrived for the promised visit, though unfortunately she could not stay long, being obliged to join the Company for their opening night at Sevastopol. They began with a performance of *Uncle Vanya*, and although the first act was received coldly, towards the end of the performance the players received a great ovation. Tchehov, who watched the play from the Director's box, was also given a wonderful reception and received many congratulations.

From Sevastopol the Company went on to Yalta, where many Russian celebrities in the world of art, literature and music had gathered to meet them. Tchehov visited the theatre daily and was in the highest spirits. He liked to arrive at the theatre very early, so that he could watch the scenery being erected. He also enjoyed watching the actors put on their make-up.

On these occasions Stanislavsky did not forget the real purpose of his visit, and with the charm which only he knew how to use, he would ask pleadingly, "When are you going to give us a new play? You have promised one, you know." Indeed, it meant so much to the Company. But Tchehov, without even the suggestion of a smile, would produce a tiny scrap of paper covered with fine thin writing. "Here it is," he would say. "Here is your new play." Then he would roar with laughter.

During that week the members of the Art Theatre Company were constantly at Tchehov's house. There was a succession of parties, and the place was thronged with guests all day. As one group finished a meal, another took their places. And in addition to the members of the company, there were many authors, including Gorky, Mamim and Bunin. Gorky, with his bright, childish smile, graceful figure and colourful picturesque speech, was a great favourite. He told the most thrilling stories of his wanderings in Russia, and his devotion to his host was unmistakable. Tchehov went from one to the other of his guests, talking and joking, and his charming infectious laugh rang through the house. These were the people he loved. They understood him; they spoke his language.

But that short week passed all too quickly, and when the Company returned to Moscow Tchehov was desperately lonely; it was impossible for him to return with them, as the doctors had forbidden it. Not until ten days later, in fact, was he able to wring permission from them to make the long journey to Moscow. And there, unfortunately, the weather was so bad that he was not able to stay long. Stanislavsky, however, refused to allow him to leave until he had promised to write a new play to add to their repertoire. This eventually became *The Three Sisters*.

Back in Yalta, Tchehov started to work in earnest on the play; he planned out the acts and carefully built up the characters. But drive himself as he would, he could make little progress. His mind was in a ferment, and he was hopelessly and irrevocably in love with Olga, for here at last was the woman he had been searching for all his life. Yet what had he to offer? Only love and devotion. She was just beginning her stage career, and to ask her to renounce this for marriage was unthinkable. They were devoted to each other, but marriage meant more than that. He had been warned that the only hope of a restoration to health was to live permanently in Yalta. The Art Theatre Company, however, belonged to Moscow, many, many miles away, so if he and Olga decided to marry they would rarely be able to live together.

Indeed, to be desperately in love at his age was extremely disturbing. It led to impulses which were hard to explain. One evening, therefore, he rang up his great friend Bunin and suggested a drive. The time was nine o'clock, and even Bunin was a little startled. "A drive! At this time of night! What's the matter?"

"I am in love," confessed Tchehov. "Let us drive to Oriana."

The night was warm and still, with a bright moon; a few stars twinkled in the dark-blue sky. The carriage rolled softly along the white road, past the sea, and then at length through the forest, laced with black shadows. Dark rows of tall cypresses towered against the sky; the ruins of the castle glimmered in the moonlight, and it was all very beautiful; so the two men got out, walked a little, and then sat down on a bench.

"You are sad to-night", said Bunin gently, for his companion was strangely silent. Surely Tchehov would reveal the reason for this sudden nocturnal expedition! Surely he was about to make a romantic confession! Bunin was only too anxious to help and advise . . . But Tchehov merely laughed and said, "It's you who are sad because you've spent so much on the cab." Well, one should never be surprised at anything Tchehov said. His humour was constantly breaking out at the most unexpected moments; that was part of his charm.

Nevertheless, love was rapidly winding him round and round with her silken threads, and in his letters he poured out all his thoughts to Olga. And now he wrote to her as a lover. She, in return, asked when they were going to meet again.

"My darling, I don't know when I am coming to Moscow", he replied. The play must be finished first, and he hoped to complete it in September, but he was "horribly and cruelly hindered by visitors". No sooner had he sat down to write than "some ugly face peeped in. I can't refuse to see people," he said. "I am not equal to it."

Even in the garden he was not free from visitors, for they would boldly enter and engage him in conversation. Beggars, students and newspaper men would arrive almost hourly, and admiring young girls would stand for hours outside his house, peering into the garden, hoping to catch a glimpse of the celebrated author. Some of his visitors would even demand an interview and begin at once to lecture him; they wished to direct his genius into what they considered was the proper path. And although Arseny, the porter, did his best to discriminate between welcome and unwelcome guests, his task was a difficult one, as the unwelcome visitors adopted various ruses with which to catch the kind-hearted author. But he, too, could be cunning at times, and sometimes as they approached he would raise his binoculars and gaze fixedly out to sea—a device that was generally highly successful.

Meanwhile, the play grew very slowly, as there were days when he was quite incapable of work. The manuscript would lie on his desk untouched for perhaps a week. This loss of time grieved him, as he felt that a play ought to be written quickly, "without taking breath". It should be set down while the inspiration was fresh and vivid. Oh, how tedious it was to be ill!

However, the first act of *The Three Sisters* was sent off to Stanislavsky. The second and third acts were to follow as soon as they were finished, and Tchehov hoped to bring the fourth act to Moscow himself.

But October arrived, and the play was still unfinished. Olga, in Moscow, was getting anxious. "Why don't you come, Anton?" she wrote. "What's keeping you." But Tchehov was not well enough to leave Yalta. Ah, how he raged at the fate which so stubbornly resisted his efforts to work!

On October 16th the play was finished, and a week later Tchehov went to Moscow, bringing the last act with him. Stanislavsky was enchanted with the play, and a reading was arranged at the theatre, after which *The Three Sisters* was discussed by the whole Company. But to Tchehov's surprise he realised that some of the actors regarded the play as a tragedy and felt that it should be played on a very gloomy and serious note. This had never been the author's intention.

On the following day rehearsals started, and to Stanislavsky the piece seemed long and tiresome. He spared no pains, and was prepared to work on the production for months, if necessary, in order to achieve "the creation of complete artistic unity" but *The Three Sisters* would not come to life. The actors rehearsed to the point of exhaustion, and Tchehov was appealed to for advice again and again, but as on previous occasions he simply could not discuss his own work. To him the whole thing was so true, so simple. He would shake his head and say, "But it is all there. I wrote it down," or he would endeavour to relieve the tension with a joke; he would take from his pocket five copecks and show them to the Company. "I received from *The Seagull* just so much," he would say, and would shake with laughter.

Yet at these rehearsals Tchehov conducted himself with extraordinary modesty. He invariably refused to sit at the Directors' table, and would seat himself almost unnoticed somewhere at the back of the stalls. Stanislavsky had had considerable experience of dramatists, and had often found them autocratic and difficult to a degree. Tchehov behaved in exactly the opposite way. In matters of art he was absolutely inflexible; nothing could shake him, but in all other matters he was willing to give way.

The rehearsals of *The Three Sisters* almost reduced Stanislavsky to despair. Then suddenly one evening he saw where the production failed; it was too gloomy. He immediately went on to the stage and showed the actors just what should be done. And from that moment the play began to live.

The idea of *The Three Sisters* had apparently been simmering in Tchehov's mind for years, and almost certainly dates back to that holiday in the country at Soumy, where, as a young man, he had been entertained by the Lintvariov family, who owned an old signorial estate. Here were three daughters, charming, intellectual and high-minded. Two were doctors, and the eldest was blind, owing to a tumour on the brain. She was often in pain, and her end could not be far off, yet she joked continually, and spoke with amazing coolness of her own approaching death. The youngest sister was "a vigorous sunburnt girl", gay, eager, affectionate, and "a passionate little Russian patriot".

There can be no doubt that *The Three Sisters* was inspired by these three girls. They were the first "daughters of the squire" Anton had ever known intimately, and his friendship with them came at a time when he was young and impressionable. These girls were fresh and eager for life, eager to be of service to humanity, and longing to take part in any cultural movement, particularly in the cause of the peasants. There were hundreds of such women in Russia at that time, caught up in the vast altruistic crusade which had been stimulated by the ancient laws of serfdom, the tyranny of the Government, and the great literature of the time.

In his play, however, Tchehov linked these girls with another memory—the country holiday he had spent at Voskressensk, when his brother Ivan had been tutor to Colonel Mayevsky's children. Anton had become friendly with many of the officers, and he himself had been an interested spectator of the love affairs which inevitably developed between the officers and the young girls of the town. To them these young men were a godsend. With their martial air and their fine uniforms they turned one pretty head after another. But not all these love affairs were simple; some were pitifully difficult to resolve. There was love in abundance, but it was not always reciprocated. Some of the officers, too, were married, but nevertheless they formed attachments. And then came the inevitable day when the battery was moved to another town; the partings were sad, indeed; some were heartbreaking.

Such was the theme of the play, and it was unfolded with exquisite tenderness and understanding. The sisters are orphans. They are on the threshhold of life, which seems to them marvellous in its opportunities for service and happiness. But they have no one to guide them, and as life's ugly problems arise they are utterly bewildered; they don't know where to turn. They cling pitifully together for support, yet each one is really alone ... alone ... The feeling of isolation is terrible, and as barriers inevitably arise between them, their little worlds spin with perplexity. How, for instance, should a young and innocent girl understand the love of an adored elder sister for a married man? Sex in the young girl is dormant; she is a virgin even in thought. But the older woman is awake and ready; the ancient primitive instinct is as undeniable as a mountain cataract roaring and rushing to the sea. It cannot be stopped or turned aside by platitudes, or notions of honour; its demands are insistent, urgent. And love is here for the taking—a dream, an enchantment; it is what one was created for, this loving and giving, this marvellous self-abasement.

But while these hearts are breaking, the uninterested spectators, totally unaware of the sadness and the yearning, are deeply engrossed in their own insignificant affairs. One man spends most of his time reading the newspaper and commenting on the petty topics of the day. Another is deeply concerned by the discovery that his hair is falling out! This is life, and the pattern has been the same for thousands of years.

Yet what is perhaps most significant in this play is the three sisters' longing for Moscow, the glittering city of their dreams. There, they believe, happiness will descend upon them like a shining cloak; when they can get away from this dreary country town, all their marvellous visions will materialise. They do not realise, they cannot know, that happiness does not depend upon place, or wealth, or even love. They cannot see that happiness is like a garden; the soil will only yield just as much as has been put into it. "Unless the jug is filled, there is nothing to pour out."

Yet from this rather sad play, there emerged a genuine note of hope, and it was expressed by Colonel Vershinin:— "It goes without saying that you cannot conquer the mass of darkness round you; little by little, as you go on living, you will be lost in the crowd . . . Life will get the better of you, but still you will not disappear without a trace. After you there may appear, perhaps, six like you, then twelve and so on, until such as you form a majority. In two or

L

three hundred years life on earth will be unimaginably beautiful, marvellous. Man needs such a life, and though he hasn't it yet, he must have a presentiment of it, expect it, dream of it, prepare for it . . ."

This was Tchehov's answer to those critics who insisted that he was a pessimist. There was hope, indeed, but man must work for it, incessantly, tirelessly; and the reward would come, if not in our lifetime, then in the future.

But Tchehov had found the discussions and re-hearsals of his play too harrowing, so in the first week of December he fled from Moscow and went to Nice. As before, he stayed at the Pension Russe, and almost im-mediately he began to write. But although he had fled from Moscow, the fortunes of the Company were never far from his thoughts, and in his letters to Olga he begged her to describe at least one rehearsal of *The Three Sisters*. His affection for her, too, was absolutely unchanged. "I often dream of you," he wrote, "and when I shut my eyes I see you although I'm awake . . . Take care of yourself, darling, and God keep you. Be a good girl, work hard and come here in the Spring."

Spring, however, was far distant, and in the meantime life in Nice had become as complicated as life in Yalta. He was recognised everywhere, and many demands were made upon his time. New acquaintances crowded upon him daily, and soon they had become even more numerous than in Moscow or Yalta. One day he was presented with an enormous bouquet. There seemed to be no place in which he could hide.

His one idea now was to work hard so that he need not write during the summer, which he hoped to spend with Olga. He wanted to go away with her to some quiet place where they could be quite alone. Would that be possible? He fervently hoped it would. Yet often he wondered if she could continue to care for him. She was surrounded by admirers and was continually meeting other men. "I love you," wrote Tchehov, "but that you don't understand . . . You need a husband, or to be more accurate a spouse ... and what am I? I'm no great shakes."

He was intensely interested in her acting, and for her part of Masha in *The Three Sisters* he gave her some valuable advice. "Don't make a mournful face in a single act," he said. "People who have borne a grief in their hearts for a long time and are used to it only whistle and often sink into thought."

The Three Sisters was presented to the public for the first time on 31st January, 1901, and although at this performance the play was not perhaps fully appreciated, yet at the second performance the audience were "spellbound". It is recorded that men and women were so moved that sounds of weeping could be heard all over the theatre. "I was not ashamed of my tears", said one critic. Unfortunately, owing to a misdirection of letters, Tchehov heard very little about the play until his return to Russia.

Chapter 25

Marriage to Olga Knipper

TCHEHOV arrived back in Russia in February, and during that Spring, which was an exceptionally warm one, he spent most of his time in his garden. Indeed, he declared that he had "given up literature", and as for play-writing he vowed that he would never write for the theatre again. Dramatic authors were treated well in countries like Germany or Sweden or Spain, but he felt that in Russia they were not treated fairly. They were abused and were not forgiven either for their successes or failures. "For one sensible person there are a thousand fools," he wrote in his notebook, "and for one sensible word there are a thousand stupid ones; the thousand overwhelm the one and that is why cities and villages progress so slowly. The majority, the mass, always remain stupid; it will always overwhelm."

But though he protested that he had abandoned literature, yet "from old habit" he wrote a story occasionally, and that beautiful story *The Bishop* was written at this time. The subject was one which had been haunting him for fifteen years, but *The Bishop* was probably written as the result of his acquaintance with a young bishop who had been an undergraduate at Moscow University in Tchehov's time.

Yet, though Tchehov was devoting little time to literature, he was working hard to complete the library he had formed at Taganrog. He was also engaged in the valuable work of assisting the invalids of Yalta. As he himself was suffering from Tuberculosis, patients from all over Russia were continually appealing to him for assistance. Doctors in Moscow, too, frequently sent patients to him with the request that he would find lodgings and make arrangements for them. Tchehov exerted himself on behalf of each one; he printed appeals in the newspapers, and in addition expended many sums out of his own pocket. But Yalta was already overcrowded with sick people, and the hotels and lodging houses often refused to take in those who were seriously ill. These people were generally very poor, and most of those who came ended their lives under wretched conditions, pining for their native place. Patients who insisted on coming to Yalta were a great anxiety to him.

His dream, one day, was to build a sanatorium for invalid village teachers; he wanted to put up a large bright building with many windows and lofty rooms, a place that could contain a fine library, lecture rooms and music. There should be a vegetable garden and orchard, there would be lectures on Agriculture, Meteorology and so on. Tchehov was keenly interested in education, and he and his friend, Gorky, the author, were continually planning improvements for schools. "Whenever I meet a teacher I feel ashamed for him," said Tchehov. "I feel ashamed for his timidity and because he is badly dressed . . . It seems to me that for the teacher's wretchedness I am myself to blame."

The village teacher in Russia at that time was, indeed, disgracefully underpaid and was accorded little or no respect from the people of the village. The village constable, the rich shop-keeper, the priest, the school guardian, the councillor and the school inspector all looked down on him and humiliated him, and for eight or nine months of the year he was obliged to live like a hermit, without books or amusements. Terrified by the fear of losing his employment, he became crushed and timid. Yet Tchehov believed that the right kind of teacher could have done much for Russia. He, in particular, could influence the individual. "I believe in individual people," said Tchehov. "I see salvation in individual personalities scattered here and there all over Russia—educated people or peasants; they have strength though they are few."

Tchehov and Olga were now discussing plans for

their marriage, for although he had thought it unwise, owing to the precarious state of his health, he realised that Olga's position was becoming difficult. He and she were constantly the subject of gossip. He was convinced that he ought not to ask any woman to share his life, nor was he fit at this stage to be the father of a family. He knew it, and as a doctor, felt very strongly about it. On the other hand, Olga had declared that as people were talking, she wished (as she said) "to regularise" her relations with him. "Please understand", she had written . . . "that I can't go through with it any more. Please believe me. You don't seem to understand this and I find it hard to talk about it. You remember how difficult it was last summer, how painful. And why do we have to do it? People are much more likely to leave us in peace and to stop talking about us if they realise that it is an accomplished fact. And it will be better for both of us too . . ." She had written also, "I am tired of this game of hide and seek. I can't bear the thought of having to watch your mother's suffering again, of having to see Marie's bewildered face again . . . It's awful. I feel as if I were between two fires at your house . . ."

So it was decided, and they planned to arrange their wedding as soon as the theatrical season ended. But the idea of a fashionable wedding was repugnant to both, so Tchehov suggested that they should be married in church and then drive straight to Svenigorod, a very beautiful monastery and town near Moscow. And for their honeymoon he suggested a trip down the Volga. But he emphasized that everything was to be as she desired; he wished only to do what would please her. "You must think about the future; you manage for me," he wrote. "I'll do as you tell me; otherwise we shall never live. We shall go on sipping life, a teaspoonful once an hour."

There was another point on which he had insisted. Before their marriage he had decided to go to Moscow and undergo a thorough medical examination. This took place in the Spring, and the specialist diagnosed "congestion in both lungs" and advised either a visit to Switzerland or a "koumiss" cure at Axyonovo. Tchehov decided to take the koumiss cure, but he and Olga wished to be married first. They therefore slipped away secretly and were married quite privately at a small Moscow church on May 25th, 1901. They skilfully avoided all publicity, and only four witnesses were present. After the ceremony they drove straight to Axyonovo, by way of the Volga, the Kama and the White River.

The sanatorium stood in a beautiful oak forest, and Tchehov was at first delighted with the place, but the life was so primitive that he soon became tired of it all. They left, therefore, before the end of the prescribed six weeks and returned to Yalta by way of Samara, down the Volga to Tsaritsyn and then to Novorossiisk. They were extremely happy. "My wife is well", wrote Tchehov to his sister, "and laughs continually." They spent the rest of the summer together in Yalta, and in the third week of August Olga returned to Moscow. They had agreed that she should continue her work on the stage, for Tchehov felt that she could not be expected to share his life in Yalta, a rather dull, provincial town filled with the aged and invalids. It was no place for a young and beautiful actress at the height of her career.

The leave-taking between Tchehov and his wife was a sad one, and when Olga had gone, Tchehov was almost overcome by his isolation and loneliness. "My dear, my darling, my good wife," he wrote, "I love you very much and will love you . . . It is so still and lonely in your room downstairs . . . Write, write, write, every day. I miss you fearfully, my angel . . . I have grown used to you like a little child and I feel cold and comfortless without you."

It was ironical, indeed, that he had been so long in finding a wife, yet now that this adorable woman was his they could not be together. Yet he had no regrets and no complaints; he was fervently grateful for the wonderful happiness she had brought him. On the other hand, she seemed to be utterly blind to his difficulties. She apparently believed that he could churn out a masterpiece at a moment's notice and did not realise that he was really an invalid, with possibly only a few years to live; it was only by a determined effort of will that he could write at all. In one of her first letters, therefore, she wrote naively, "Anton, you must now write something new. There are so many subjects in your head. Don't be lazy, darling, do make an effort and write." An effort, indeed! His whole life had been one long strenuous effort, a constant and desperate struggle. Four days later she wrote again, "Anton, write something; I can hardly wait for the time when I shall read your new story. Write, darling; it will help to while away the time of our separation." Again, three days later, she urged him to "Work, darling, work," and a week later, "Write, Anton darling. I shall tremble with excitement when I read something new you have written."

Was ever any woman so blind and yet so fond? For to accuse him of laziness was cruel and unjust; it was the very last fault of which he could be accused. Yet she continued:—"Darling, you will let me know what you are writing, won't you?" And five days later, "Darling, don't you feel any pleasure in being able to write? Doesn't it thrill you? You are my great genius. You are the Russian Maupassant . . . Don't give way to melancholy. Write something more for me and for Russia." A week later she was urging him once more:—"Anton, darling, you must write a comedy; it will create a sensation; there are no Russian comedies." And so it went on; almost every letter was in the same strain.

Meanwhile, there were days when he had barely strength to dress himself, or hold a pen, let alone produce creative literature, a task which can be more exhausting than the heaviest physical work. Had she never been told that a book is composed with blood and sweat and tears? That it is not a gift, but infinite labour? As for laziness, had he not sat at his desk, day after day, month after month, year after year, at all hours, writing, eternally writing, until his head spun? All his life he had worked, under the most difficult conditions, like a galley-slave. He had struggled against poverty and ill-health until he was worn out; there was nothing left. Yet the woman he loved was foolish enough to imagine that great literature could be written by a wave of the hand. "You possess", she said, "such a rich store of material and observations that all you have to do is to sit down at your desk for a short time and something beautiful is sure to emerge." Merciful heavens, how little she knew! Could she not realise that no great work had ever been produced in that way? Did not she herself, as an actress, have to work and strive for months for perfection?

Perhaps the truth was that as she had married a famous author she wanted to have something to show for it. Perhaps she imagined that she could inspire him, he who had given his life to Literature and was almost burnt out. The foolish urgent letters, however, still came:—"Darling Anton, are you going to start work or not? Please make a little effort. Surely your time will pass more quickly if you are writing. Don't you think so? I know you will write something nice, elegant, elegant in form, of course. I feel terribly excited about it already."

Well, there it was. That was Olga, and she was really no different from many other foolish and impulsive women; he had known them as patients. How could she be expected to understand? And as a matter of fact he did not wish her to know that he lay awake, night after night, coughing and sweating, that his headaches and palpitations were sometimes unbearable; he did not wish her to know. Better to put on a brave face, to smile, and make jokes, and so keep her love. She liked everything round her to be gay and merry, and it was his duty to keep her happy.

Olga complained, however, that he did not confide in her, that he did not tell her all his thoughts. She wanted to know everything; she wanted him to pour out his soul to her. As if that were possible! No, even at the risk of displeasing her he had to admit that that was not his way. How could he confess that sometimes he felt near to death? She could not save him, and it would only distress her.

Better to keep her in that fool's paradise, for she could not possibly work happily at the theatre (which she adored) if she was constantly anxious about him. And without her work as an actress she would have been miserable; she could never have stood the life in Yalta.

Yalta was now at the height of its fashionable season, and many celebrities were staying there. Most of them were acquainted with Tchehov, and visitors came continually to his house. Kuprin, Bunin, Karabtchevsky, Orlenev, Elpatyevsky and Gorky were constant visitors. Tolstoy, too, was staying near Yalta at this time, and Tchehov paid several visits to him. The old man had been ill but was now convalescent. He had become very attached to Tchehov and thought him "a beautiful, magnificent man" and an "incomparable artist".

But this Tchehov was a very different man from the author who had visited Yasnaya Polyana some years before; and Tolstoy must have noticed it. Tchehov's voice, which only a few years ago had held the vigour and resonance of youth, had become tired and husky, and his complexion, which tanned so readily, had grown sallow. His love of fun and his sense of humour were as strong as ever, yet obviously the fire in him was slowly dying. He walked and spoke slowly, and he had grown a little absent-minded.

Tolstoy had only just realised that Tchehov was a serious dramatist, and although he had read his plays with interest, he did not really appreciate or understand them; and one day as he was saying goodbye to Tchehov he remarked good-naturedly, "You are a very good fellow and I am very fond of you, and as you know I can't bear Shakespeare, but still, his plays are better than yours." How typical this was of Tolstoy! For obviously a play, in his opinion, should have a message; it should be written with a very real purpose.

Tchehov, however, did not attempt to defend his work. It was typical of him, too, that he never condemned the work of other artists, unless he felt that it was evil. He realised, in fact, how much injustice resulted from condemnation of what was only partially understood. "Lord, don't allow me to condemn or to speak of what I do not know or do not understand," he wrote in his notebook. And it was noticed that pretentious and boastful persons unconsciously became simpler and more truthful in his presence. His own simplicity and candour made them almost ashamed. Visitors, on being introduced, would sometimes attempt to discuss "deep questions", using long words and grandiloquent phrases, but Tchehov would quietly change the subject, and would draw his visitor out to speak of his own work or of matters in which he was genuinely interested. Soon they would be talking simply and naturally. Gorky has said that Tchehov was "gentleness personified" and that one simply could not imagine him arguing or losing his temper.

Many of Tchehov's visitors at this time were invalids, some of whom were extremely poor. As a result, his money disappeared with alarming rapidity; he could not refuse financial help to anyone in distress. He also received at this time more begging letters than ever before—from those who were ill or unsuccessful, and from those who were merely foolish, thriftless, lazy or criminals. And many of these people did not ask for money but *demanded* it. There were numerous letters, too, from men and women who believed themselves to be despised or persecuted. He did what he could for each one, yet he rarely received any thanks or gratitude. The only result of his generosity, as a rule, was a further demand for money.

Tchehov was also at this time collecting subscriptions towards a plan (originated by Dr. Altshuller) for building a sanatorium in Yalta, a scheme which was very near to his heart.

Chapter 26

Life in Yalta

O N September 16th, 1901, Tchehov went to Moscow for ten days, and was present at some rehearsals, but on his return to Yalta he again found it very difficult to settle down. Without his wife, life was wretchedly incomplete. "I live like a monk and dream only of you," he wrote to her. "Though it's a disgrace to be making declarations of love at forty, yet I cannot refrain from telling you once more that I love you deeply and tenderly." And now for the first time in his letters he spoke of children. Apparently she was anxious to have a child, and he was convinced that it would make her life happier and more complete. It was clear, in fact, that Olga was not really happy. Her capriciousness, extreme sensitivity and moodiness were obviously the result of those strong maternal longings which few women are able to sublimate. "I have thought you need a little son who would occupy you and fill up your life," wrote Tchehov. "You *will* have a little son or daughter, my own, believe me; you need only wait a little," he said.

Did he not remember those peasant women whom he had attended in childbirth? Would he ever forget the wonderful expression of happiness on their faces when the child was born? It was the loveliest sight in the world to see a woman so deliriously happy, as she took her baby into her arms, and every time he had seen it he had marvelled afresh.

But Olga at this time was torn between her love for her husband and her work. Often she felt that she was being utterly selfish in not living with him. His health was poor and she realised that he was very lonely. Yet he could not and would not advise her. They had agreed, at the time of their marriage, that she should continue her stage career, and the decision to alter that must now rest with her. He knew that she was passionately fond of her work, and he realised that life in Yalta would be dull for a woman of her temperament. Yet it was inevitable that he should often wonder if they were wise in living apart. His letters to her did not always satisfy him. "After what you and I have lived through together letters are not enough," he wrote. "We ought to go on living; we are so wrong in not living together. But there, what is the use of talking of it? . . . I bless you, my little German and I rejoice that you are in good spirits."

The weather in Yalta was beautiful now, although the month was November. Roses, pinks and chrysanthemums were still in flower in Tchehov's garden, and on many days he was able to sit outdoors. He had started to write again, but not with any real enthusiasm, and he never now attempted to hurry over his work. Stanislavsky and Nemirovitch were urging him to write another play, but he could make no promises; he could only say that possibly in the Spring he might make an effort in that direction. Indeed, on reflection, writing for the theatre brought many irritations. *The Three Sisters*, for instance, had just been produced in Yalta by some obscure actor-manager, and the performance had been "revolting", with the result that the audience had abused the play dreadfully. The producer had consulted Tchehov beforehand in order to secure his co-operation, and Tchehov had begged him not to produce the play. Writing for the Moscow Art Theatre was, of course, a very different proposition because they had evolved a special technique which was exactly suited to his work, and they took infinite pains with every production. But apart from all other considerations, the actual writing had latterly become very exhausting. There were so many days on which he was incapable of any effort, and to pick up the threads again after an interval was hard labour.

Tchehov's health, as a matter of fact, showed little real improvement, and the disease itself made him extremely restless. His isolation from Moscow and his separation from his wife were two griefs to which he could not resign himself. Between her visits he merely existed, and life began again for him only when they were together. The uncertainty of her visits, too, caused him much anxiety, for she could never make definite plans until the very last moment, and he went through agonies of alternate expectations and disappointments. When she wrote to say that she would soon be coming to Yalta he was as happy as a child again, but in the next letter she would plunge him into misery; she was not certain that she could come. Then finally circumstances would prevent the visit. He made brave attempts to adopt a fatalistic attitude to whatever might happen, but the fact remained that she was the very centre of his existence. No one else could take her place.

Tchehov's mother was now over eighty, and although she still supervised the housekeeping, she was not really equal to the task. To arrange her son's diet (which should, of course, have been a very carefully planned one) was beyond her, and the old servant ("Granny") who had been with the family for many years, was now seventy years old; she, too, was incapable of making proper arrangements for the invalid. Tchehov at this time kept two maid-servants and a man-servant, yet there was little comfort in the house. His study was often cold, as the stoves were badly managed, and he was rarely given the food he needed.

"I am awfully worried at your being cold," wrote Olga, and she begged him to "act vigorously", to give orders and insist on his room being warm. Tchehov, stirred to action by this advice, did endeavour to remedy matters, but it was quite useless; his mother and "Granny" were devoted to him and he could not criticise them. He told Olga, therefore, that when she came all would be well; she could rearrange everything and see that he was made more comfortable. "Every day I think of how you will come," he wrote, "and how we shall spend three days together." (He was expecting her for Christmas.) "How delighted I should be now to talk a little with my wife, to

touch her on the brow and the shoulders, to laugh with her!"
"Ah, darling, darling . . . Do come, my sweet, I entreat
you," he said. "I am very dreary, so dreary that I can't
work at all and only sit and read the newspaper . . ."

Tchehov, indeed, decided that whatever happened
he would never spend another winter in Yalta. In spite of
all that the doctors could say he would go to Moscow. He
would not stay on what he called this "Devils Island".

Olga, in the meantime, was living in a whirl of gaiety.
She was attending dinners and jubilees, and often she did
not go to bed until early morning. "Ah, how I envy you,"
wrote Tchehov. "I envy your vigour, your freshness, your
health, your temperament . . . In the old days I could
drink with anyone, as the saying is."

Chapter 27

"The Cherry Orchard"

ON December 10th, 1901, Tchehov became so seriously ill that the news was sent to Olga. But the sick man begged her not to be anxious about him; he insisted that this was merely a slight relapse from which he would soon recover. He had now become resigned to the fact that she would be unable to come to Yalta for Christmas. "And, indeed," he wrote, "you had better not come here, my darling. Do your work and we shall still have time to be together."

Very slowly he got well, but he was extremely weak for some time, and suffered badly from insomnia. Ah, those long and lonely nights! But with the first light he grew calmer, and memories of the past would come crowding upon him, memories of Taganrog—the house in Monastery Street, the Cathedral, the religious processions. He was walking again with the choir-boys, singing and chanting; he was following the banners and the ikons . . . "Holy, holy, holy!" sang the childish voices . . . He remembered again the Polish family who had been so kind to him in his loneliness. Alas, tragedy had overtaken them. The father had brought disgrace and poverty upon the family, the elder daughter had married a rascal, the son (a promising medical student) had died of tuberculosis. In the old days they had been such a delightful family.

He remembered, too, walking in the Dubki woods near Taganrog on May days, gathering flowers and the lovely green boughs. Thoughts of Bogimovo, too, were never far away; he was back again sitting on the verandah with the lovely Lika laughing up at him. Dear, enchanting Lika! Apparently she had grown fat and become dignified . .

He remembered, too, Levitan, the painter, so gay, so talented, and unfortunately so impressionable. He had been one of the best landscape painters in Russia, but women had worn him out. "The dear creatures give love," said Tchehov, "but they take from man quite a trifle, only his youth. It is impossible to paint a landscape without pathos, without ecstasy, and ecstasy is impossible when one has gorged oneself . . . If I were a landscape painter I would lead a life almost ascetic . . ." So much for Levitan.

Surely it was sentimental and weak to indulge in these nostalgic reflections! But the past seemed so beautiful, and his isolation craved for such comfort. He had uprooted himself, and he felt that he could never take root in Yalta.

Visitors, during this illness, were very kind, but without Olga he felt utterly helpless and lonely. "Without you", he wrote, "I am good for nothing."

Marie came to Yalta for Christmas, and she immediately took charge of the domestic arrangements, and supervised his diet. Olga, alas, did not come. "When, when shall we see each other?" demanded Tchehov, yet never once did he reproach her, nor did he begrudge her her parties and gaiety. He begged her to be "well, merry, happy. Don't be faithless to your husband if you can help it," he wrote. "I am not faithless to you, and, indeed, I couldn't be, my joy."

At the beginning of January Tchehov was able to go outdoors for the first time since his illness; his health had improved and he declared that he was growing stronger every day. Now, indeed, spring did not seem so far away, for already the birds were singing, and the weather was warm and sunny. In a burst of creative activity he felt a sudden desire to write, and a new play gradually took shape in his mind. It came, as he said, "like the first streak of sunrise" and he did not know, as yet, whether any good would come of it. But the joy of creation was with him again, and he wrote with real enthusiasm. Would not Olga, too, be pleased, as the Company were always clamouring for a new play? He could refuse nothing to Olga.

In his new house he had arranged a charming room as his study. It was both light and sunny and was well furnished with many books, an oriental carpet and tasteful furniture. The walls were hung with portraits of Tolstoy, Turgenev and Grigorovitch, there were photographs of actors and authors, and above the brown, dutch-tiled fireplace hung a picture of a moonlit hayfield painted by Levitan. In this room he would work, as a rule, until midday, but after lunch, on fine days he would walk in the garden for a short time, accompanied by his two devoted dogs, Tusik and Kashtan. The distant sea, with its pretty sailing-boats, was fascinating to contemplate. But what he loved most was the evening sky; to see the sun set, and watch the rosy light flood the horizon and paint the clouds with gold, was a perpetual delight; he never tired of it. But twilight, too, was a joy, and he loved to watch the bats, in their queer, gliding dance . . . As darkness fell, an owl would cry out from the old cypresses, a faint scent of mignonette drifted in from the garden, and the stars would appear in the dark-blue sky. He had always loved the night, with its silence, its shadows, its floating moon. "The sense of beauty in man knows no bounds," he had written years ago. And beauty was still capable of wrapping itself round his heart.

On fine days Tchehov would stroll down to the sea, and on one such occasion he was approached by a young naval officer. "Are you Anton Pavlovitch Tchehov?" the young man asked shyly. "Ah, I have long wanted to shake you by the hand." He was a handsome youth, with a very fine face, and Tchehov was delighted with this spontaneous greeting.

Tchehov, indeed, loved young people at this time. He understood them, too, as few middle-aged men could. "Only those young people can be accepted as healthy who refuse to be reconciled with the old order, and foolishly or wisely struggle against it," he declared. "Such is the will of nature and the foundation of progress." But he had strong views as to work, especially with regard to the young author. "A writer must work very hard," he maintained; "he ought to work every day without fail." "But for God's sake don't read your work to anyone until it is published," he said to Kuprin. "Don't read it to others, even in proof."

And most strongly of all did he insist that an author must be courageous. "It is important never to take any-one's advice," he said. "If you have made a mess of it, let the blood be on your own head." As to the actual craft of fiction, Tchehov's views had changed very little since he had given advice to his brother, Alexander, many years before:—"Don't give your hands liberty when your brain is lazy. Work should be work. Don't invent sufferings you have not experienced and don't paint pictures you have not seen, for a lie in a story is much more boring than a lie in conversation." He had always insisted, also, that an author should avoid describing the psychological state of the charac-ters, but should contrive that this became clear from their actions. His view on vulgar publicity, too, was that "Real talent keeps always in obscurity, among the crowd, far from the show."

Remembering his own youth, Tchehov was particu-larly kind to young writers, and if they were discouraged he would remind them that "Individuals do not dominate, but their work is apparent". Aspiring authors frequently sent manuscripts for him to read and advise upon, and the telephone rang continually asking for interviews. He did what he could for each one, although these people had no claim on him whatever. Did he not remember what valuable advice and help he had received as a young man, from Suvorin, Grigorovitch and others? He remembered also his friend Popudoglo (dead and buried long ago) who, as a veteran author, had taught him much. He had spent many an evening with the old drunkard, poring over books, and some of his excellent advice he remembered with gratitude even to-day. Such men were dear to beginners.

Indeed, sometimes Tchehov would come upon a young author of real promise, and it was like "heavenly manna" even to talk to him. For disillusionment had not

arrived, and Literature was believed to be a holy and
blessed profession. Dear me, he would be disillusioned soon
enough. But the young enthusiasm, the thirst for knowledge,
the bright hopes, were very refreshing.

To one such writer, who confessed that he had to
work under very difficult conditions, Tchehov generously
offered the use of a room in his house. "And I hope you
will dine with me, too," he said. He also offered to read
the work or see the proofs. "Do not waste your youth and
elasticity," he advised kindly. "Now is the time for work."

On the other hand, sometimes a huge manuscript
would be sent to Tchehov for criticism, which revealed not
the slightest sign of talent. The work was positively painful
to read; it was hopelessly banal. Yet what could one say?
It was so cruel to crush the eager hopes of a young author,
though perhaps it was even more cruel to encourage him
with false praise.

Olga arrived in Yalta at the end of February for a
stay of five days, and after her departure Tchehov began
to make plans for the coming summer. His dream was to
take a small furnished house on the Volga, one with a
sheltered garden, near a harbour, if possible. "It would
be nice", he wrote to Olga, "to have a little lodge where you
could do the housekeeping, and I could give you orders
and be very exacting." Unfortunately, however, Olga had
a miscarriage at the beginning of April and was laid up
in Petersburg for two weeks. When she was able to travel
she came to Yalta, where Tchehov himself nursed her; but
the hottest weeks were spent together in a small lodge lent
by Stanislavsky, at Lyubimovka, about eighteen miles from
Moscow; then in August Tchehov returned to Yalta to
resume work on his new play. His doctor, incidentally,
assured him that his health was steadily improving, and to
judge by the change which had taken place since the
Spring, the disease was being cured.

So already Tchehov began to make happy plans. He
would go to Moscow in October, and there he would do
nothing but eat, drink, sleep, go to the theatre and be nice

to his wife. "And so we shall soon see each other, my little beetle," he wrote. "I shall come and stay with you until you turn me out." But he warned Olga that his clothes were very shabby, so perhaps it would be wiser not to recognise him when he arrived. "Instead of saying "How do you do" at the station, I shall just give you a wink," he said quaintly.

He went to Moscow on October 12th, and stayed there for about six weeks, meeting friends and being entertained. There was also much that was new to see in connection with the Moscow Art Theatre Company, as great changes had taken place since his last visit. Owing to the generosity of S. T. Morozov, a rich man who had become keenly interested in the Company, the theatre had been entirely rebuilt and refurnished. Morozov had done this without any thought of personal gain, and entirely at his own expense. The work had taken several months, and included a revolving stage, a device which was quite rare at that time, even in Europe. Morozov had also put the Company on to a sound financial basis, thus relieving the Directors of a heavy burden of anxiety. There had been a financial loss, which grew with each month, so Morozov had bought up all the holdings of the shareholders.

Morozov was also particularly interested in the lighting system of the stage and auditorium, and he had taken charge of this work, frequently donning an overall and working side by side with the electricians and mechanics. In spite of his many business interests he had turned a room in his mansion into a laboratory for his electrical experiments. His unselfish devotion to the theatre, in fact, had endeared him to every member of the Company, and without his assistance the continuation of their valuable work would have been impossible.

The Company were now installed in their new theatre, of which they were all very proud, and Tchehov was as excited and happy as any schoolboy. But it was a sad moment when he was obliged to leave Moscow again. During this visit Olga had grown infinitely precious to him.

"I love you even more dearly than before," he wrote on his return. "You have spoilt me dreadfully." But he insisted that she was not to worry about him; everything was all right. He was sleeping and eating well and not coughing. As to the play (*The Cherry Orchard*), he hoped to send it in February, and in March he expected to be with her again.

Meanwhile, Olga begged to know when the play would be ready; they were all so desperately anxious to see it. Alas, Tchehov was forced to confess that he had not yet resumed work on the play, but he assured her that the moment he did so she should be told. He assured her, too, that he had not forgotten them all; every detail concerning the theatre was precious to him and he begged her to tell him all that was happening in Moscow. Only then would he feel that he was not submerged by this dreary and empty life in Yalta. "Forgive me that I am not living with you," he said, "but next year everything shall be properly arranged; I will be with you; that is certain."

Christmas came and went, but still he had not started work on the play. He was not well enough to write, nor was he in the mood. Therefore, he had "cast everything aside".

But he was already making plans for the summer. Instead of taking a cottage in the country, could they not go to Switzerland? He had never been there before, but if Olga agreed, they would go in May and stay there for two months. Amongst the mountains they would be quite alone. It was always so difficult to be alone with Olga; whenever they were together they were disturbed by visitors.

When at last he heard from Olga that she agreed to the trip abroad he was in ecstasies. Indeed, he felt that there was no time to be wasted, for during the last few months he had realised that life was slipping away from him. "Our youth will be gone in two or three years' time," he said sadly. "We must make haste, we must do our utmost to get something out of it . . ." So he began to make definite plans. They would spend five days in Vienna, then go to Berlin and Dresden, and from there proceed to

Switzerland. It would be "glorious" and "perfect" to be travelling together. "When are you going to take me away to Italy or Switzerland?" he asked. "I want to live." He wanted to make excursions and do some walking there, and when they were together he intended to "dance attendance" on her. Olga, for her part, assured him that she was anxious to go to Switzerland, but first she begged him to finish the play. They needed a new play so urgently. Indeed, unless he set to work soon she threatened to take him in hand. "Do take me in hand," he begged. "There is only one thing I desire—to get into your hands." Yet realising that the Company were very anxious as to the fate of the play, he assured her that he had not forgotten his promise; had he only had the strength, he would have written twenty-five plays. But for the time being they must all be patient.

By the middle of March the weather in Yalta had become really Spring-like, and Tchehov was able to walk into the town almost every day. He had grown much stronger. In April, therefore, he went to Moscow and stayed until June, but the projected trip to Switzerland did not materialise, chiefly because the weather was so hot. His doctors, too, advised him against it, and Professor Ostroumov, who examined him in May, said that he might spend the winter in the vicinity of Moscow, but somewhere in the country. For this purpose two friends offered to lend their houses, and M. Teleshov even offered to build one for the sick man. But finally Tchehov decided to remain near Moscow, and here he and Olga spent June and part of July, returning to the Crimea for the latter part of the summer.

Chapter 28

Last days

OLGA returned to Moscow in September, and after her departure Tchehov resumed work on *The Cherry Orchard*. But he wrote with little enthusiasm, for often he fancied that he had already outlived his day as a writer. "Every sentence I write strikes me as good for nothing and of no use at all," he confessed. Nevertheless, by the end of September the play was finished. It had taken longer than he had anticipated, but he had been ill, off and on, the whole time. "How hard it was for me to write it, darling!" he explained to Olga. And this cry from the heart apparently touched her. She had a guilty feeling that her place was by the side of her sick husband, and at times she reproached herself bitterly for remaining in Moscow. "There is such a horrible falseness in my life," she wrote, "that I don't know how to live . . . And here I go about desolate. I scourge myself, I blame myself on every side, I feel I am at fault all round. There is something I cannot cope with in life."

She was obviously devoted to Tchehov, but would they have been happy together if she had left the stage? She was capricious, easily offended, often unreasonable and quick-tempered. She was, in fact, very feminine. And even in her work she went through agonies of nerves if she believed that she had acted badly. Some years before, when she had played in *Uncle Vanya*, she had wept all night because she felt that she had failed. "There is such gloom, such horror in my soul that I can't describe it," she had written . . . "My God, how wretched I am! Everything is shattered."

Indeed, it is clear that this charming but neurotic woman was totally unsuited to the task of nursing a very sick man. She had no vocation for such work.

In October the finished copy of *The Cherry Orchard* was sent off to Moscow, and three weeks later Tchehov went there to assist and advise in the production. He spent many days in the theatre, he was happy and enthusiastic, and his lost energy and health had apparently returned. Indeed, he began to wonder why he had ever left Moscow; he felt so well, so strong; there was nothing he could not accomplish.

But what a difficult play *The Cherry Orchard* was! Stanislavsky knew now what to expect, yet again he was completely at a loss. The play was so delicate, poetical and profound that he was afraid to handle it. To Tchehov it was all so clear, but Stanislavsky found it the most difficult piece he had ever attempted to produce, as every line needed the exact intonation. Tchehov's theory was that acting should be "simple, profound and noble", but this was a generalisation which did not help, and Stanislavsky nearly tore his hair in desperation. There were endless discussions and rehearsals, but little progress was made, and the author and producer began to despair of achieving any real harmony.

Finally it was decided that the play should be produced for Tchehov's "Jubilee" (they were to celebrate the twenty-five years of his literary activity), then in the event of the play proving a failure, the unusual conditions of the evening could be said to be responsible.

The Cherry Orchard was presented to the public on the 17th January, 1904, and Tchehov was not present until the third act, when he arrived in response to the urgent entreaties of Stanislavsky. But on arrival he was given a great ovation, and many addresses were read in his honour. A jubilee wreath covered by a very fine embroidered cloth (which Stanislavsky had bought in Moscow as a present to the author) was also presented to him. Tchehov stood on the stage, deathly pale and thin, listening to the speeches with grave attention, but he coughed incessantly, and it was obvious that he could barely stand for weakness. Someone in the audience, therefore, suggested that he should be seated. But Tchehov continued to stand, still smiling.

The ovation, so warm, so lavish, and (to him) so unexpected, touched him deeply, but the embroidery given to him by Stanislavsky he thought a huge joke. "This is a wonderful thing," he said. "It should be kept in a museum." (He had no idea what to do with it.)

"But what should we have given you?" asked Stanislavsky, in bewilderment. "A rat trap," answered Tchehov merrily . . . "or a piece of rubber pipe . . . or socks . . . Look, my wife doesn't attend to me as she should. She is an actress, so I am obliged to walk around with holes in my socks. 'Listen, little soul,' I say to her. 'The big toe of my right foot is coming out.' 'Wear it on your left foot,' she answers." And Tchehov shook with laughter.

The Cherry Orchard, on that first night, achieved only a mediocre success, although it was acclaimed later as an exquisite piece of literature, almost inexhaustible in its profundity, and breathing the very essence of Russian poetry. It is clear, too, that this play is one which had to be written, for the idea had been in Tchehov's mind for years, ever since that holiday at Soumy, when he had visited the Smagin's estate, an ancient manor, "great and fertile, but old, neglected and dead as last year's cobwebs". Such estates were typical of what was happening at that time all over Russia, owing to the "new order", and the emancipation of the serfs. Estates were being broken up because the owners, born to wealth, could not adapt themselves to the new conditions. They had received no compensation for the loss of their serfs, and without their assistance, few landowners could manage their estates. They were therefore run at a loss, became heavily mortgaged and were finally sold.

Such was the theme, and the cherry orchard in the play was part of an old estate owned by a Madame Ranevsky, who, all her life, had been surrounded by wealth and luxury. She was a charming, but vain, shallow and stupid woman, who could not and would not realise the new order. She was bankrupt, and her estate was heavily mortgaged, yet she still played the great lady, and scattered her largesse as though she was still a rich woman. Her governess, tutor, footman and old retainers were still with her; they were old and devoted, and did not want their freedom. Madame Ranevsky had a worthless lover, whom she had left on the continent, and apparently he had deserted her for another woman, yet she was still passionately in love with him and was ready to fly back to his arms. This was woman's love. It mattered nothing to her that her servants, when the estate was sold, would have nowhere to go, that they were old and ill, that they had served faithfully for years. It mattered nothing to her that her young daughter was wretchedly unhappy because her mother had taken a lover, that the old mansion would be sold, that she had no place in this terrifying world . . . Madame Ranevsky, in fact, was determined to live as she had always done, and what could be more amusing at this time than to give a party? They would ask friends in to dance, and so forget their troubles . . .

In the meantime, a self-made merchant, Lopahin, whose father and grandfather had been slaves, was ready and anxious to buy the estate. He intended to divide it into plots on which summer villas could be built. "There used to be only the gentlefolk and the peasants in the country," he says, "but now there are these summer visitors . . . and one may say for sure that in another twenty years' time there'll be many more of these people, and that they'll be everywhere."

But the faithful old footman sees it very differently. "I don't feel well," he says. "In the old days we used to have Generals, Barons and Admirals at our balls, and now we send for the post office clerk and the station master, and even they're not over anxious to come."

Madame Ranevsky's brother is as foolish, improvident, reckless and unbusiness-like as his sister. He, too, is blind to what has happened. He has run through all his money. But is that his fault? Money slips through one's fingers. Besides, he may think of a plan to save the estate. "I keep thinking and racking my brains," he says. "I have many schemes, a great many, and that really means none. If we could only come in for a legacy from somebody, or marry our Anya to a very rich man. Or we might go to Yaroslavl and try our luck with our old aunt, the Countess. She's very, very rich, you know."

This foolish man, in fact, is more interested in the game of billiards than in the estate. (He is constantly practising imaginary shots.) He also solaces himself by incessantly eating caramels. "They say I've eaten up my property in caramels," he laughs.

So finally the estate is sold to the merchant Lopahin, and he is almost frantic with delight. "My God, the cherry orchard's mine," he cries. "Tell me that I'm drunk, that I'm out of my mind, that it's all a dream . . .

"If my father and grandfather could rise from their graves and see all that has happened! How their Yermolay, ignorant, beaten Yermolay, who used to run about barefoot in winter, how that very Yermolay has bought the finest estate in the world. I have bought the estate where my father and grandfather were slaves, where they weren't even admitted into the kitchen. I am asleep, I am dreaming . . . Hey, musicians, play! I want to hear you. Come, all of you, and look how Yermolay Lopahin will take the axe to the cherry orchard, and how the trees will fall to the ground. We will build houses on it, and our grandsons and great-grandsons will see a new life springing up there. Music! Play up!"

Madame Ranevsky, now at last brought face to face with reality, can only weep. But it is the young Anya, her seventeen-year-old daughter, who endeavours to comfort her. She whose young life has already been cruelly wounded has yet the courage to say "Don't weep, mamma. Life is still before you; you have still your good pure heart. Let us go, let us go, darling, away from here. We will make a new garden, more splendid than this one; you will see it, you will understand, and joy, quiet, deep joy will sink into your soul like the sun at evening. And you will smile, mamma. Come, darling, let us go."

In the end, therefore, Tchehov shows that it is to youth that courage belongs; it is to the young generation that one must look for a new life. As the old order changes they must march in front with the banners, and others, perhaps, will follow. The young student in the play (Trofimov) also shows his courage. "I have a foreboding of happiness, Anya," he says. "I see glimpses of it already ... It is coming nearer and nearer . . . And if we may never see it, if we may never know it, what does it matter? Others will see it afterwards."

Yet it is clear that few of the audience really understood *The Cherry Orchard* or its deeper meaning, for, as Tchehov wrote in his notebook, "The public really love in art that which is banal and long familiar, that to which they have grown accustomed." Besides, unlike so many playwrights, Tchehov had no axe to grind. To an audience, probably, that was incomprehensible. They were unconsciously looking for something to tag on to, some message, some solution, to Russia's many problems. Who can blame them? They did not realise that to have no axe to grind was something very noble, very rare.

As for the members of the Art Theatre Company, when all was over they blamed themselves for having left out much that was in the play. It was a play of infinite possibilities, and they felt that they, too, had failed.

During the celebration of the New Year, many festivities were arranged in Tchehov's honour, but all such functions weakened and tired him. So in February he returned to Yalta, and although he bore the ordeal of the journey without serious loss of strength, on his return it was obvious to his family and friends that his health was completely shattered. He himself would not admit this, however, and in April he was planning to go out to the Far East in July or August to serve in the Russo-Japanese war, as a doctor. The project was madness, of course, and it was never to materialise. He was dreaming and making plans, too, for the summer. He had decided to buy a boat (there was a shop which sold the very boat he wanted), and he also intended to try a new (English) method of fishing without bait, in which he was much interested. "I am dreaming of the summer," he said. "I am so longing to be alone, to write, to think . . ."

Meanwhile, life in Yalta was very boring and dull, and his life seemed dreary and empty. The damp was awful, and the skies were grey. "I can't exist without the theatre and literature," he confessed. Indeed, he longed to write, and there was "a mass of subjects in his head", but he had not the strength. He had also lost his appetite, and the hot Russian baths, which he adored, had been forbidden him by his doctor. They were, to the average healthy person, the most wonderful tonic, for after the first disagreeable sensation of heat had passed and one had perspired enormously, there was a feeling of the most heavenly happiness. All pain and every disagreeable sensation seemed to melt away, and one felt as light as a feather. The sluicing with cold water which followed actually heightened the sensation; one felt purified, cleansed, cleared out to the very inmost soul . . .

Yet why should Olga be bothered with his health? She could do nothing, and anxiety would merely hinder her in her work. He therefore assured her in his letters that his health was "splendid" and that he was "eating like a tiger." "I am alive, strong as a bull and in good humour," he wrote. Indeed, he almost convinced himself that this was true. Why should he not go to Moscow? The express trains had started running again, and it seemed to him that the company of his wife and his interests there would be far more beneficial than this dreary life in Yalta. He felt isolated, frustrated, like a squirrel in a cage. Oh, how he longed to stroll along the Nevsky Prospect, or along Petrovka in Moscow! How he ached to listen to good music, to sit for an hour or so in a restaurant, to attend rehearsals at the theatre!

The desire, in fact, could not be resisted, and he set off bravely on his long journey to Moscow, a distance of nearly eight hundred miles. But he was desperately ill on the way, and on arrival was obliged to take to his bed. There he remained for nearly a month, and he was in such pain that he was obliged to be drugged with morphia and heroin. This last illness, however, could not be ignored, and he was urged by his doctors to go as soon as possible to Badenweiler, in the Black Forest of Germany. In June, therefore, accompanied by Olga, he left Russia, and on arrival at Baden he declared that his health had much improved. "I am beginning to get fat, and am all day long on my legs, not lying down," he said. Indeed, in spite of his weakness, he wrote long letters to his sister. "Health is coming back to me, not by ounces, but by stones," he wrote. "The only trace of my illness is my extreme thinness."

In the meantime, he and Olga were staying at the Villa Frederike, which stood in a luxuriant garden, gay with lovely flowers. Beyond the garden could be seen the mountains, covered with forests. At seven a.m. and at midday a very expensive band played in the garden, but Tchehov considered it quite "talentless"; it gave him little pleasure. What invalid, either, cared to be wakened by a German band at seven in the morning?

From the Villa Frederike, therefore, they moved to another hotel, and from there Tchehov wrote to tell Marie that they would meet in August, or even before. "Keep well and gay," he said. And again he began to dream of the future, how soon he and Olga would go together to the Italian lakes. Then they would return to Yalta by sea from Trieste. That would be a wonderful trip and one he had long contemplated.

None of these plans was to materialise, however, for he did not improve, and on the 1st of July it was apparent that he had not long to live. That evening he declared that he was better, he chatted with Olga and even thought out a new story to amuse her. But later on, during the night, he woke up and for the first time in his life, asked to see a doctor. The doctor arrived, and ordered champagne, a drink that Tchehov could always appreciate. But even

as he lifted the glass he said calmly, "I am dying". He
then turned to Olga with a smile and said, "It's a long time
since I have drunk champagne". A little later he breathed
his last, courageous to the end.

Tchehov was buried in Moscow in the Novodyevitchy
Monastery, beside his father's grave, and about a hundred
people followed the procession, at the head of which a
stout policeman rode very pompously on a big white horse.
The mourners looked at it with sadness and distaste, for if
ever a man was simple and hated ceremony it was Tchehov.
How he would have deplored it all! Yet most of the
mourners had come out of love for this great but simple
man. He had died comparatively young, and his death was
a serious loss to literature, yet his work remained. He had
illumined the springs of human conduct with a clarity,
beauty and delicacy which had never been excelled, and
his stories would inspire whole generations of writers.
Wars and revolutions might destroy for ever the life he
had painted, but his work would survive. And those who
knew him best realised that his life also was an inspiration.
He had lived it nobly, unselfishly and with rare courage.

As for his message, could it not be found in what he
had written to a friend only a year or so before his death?—
"Modern culture is but the beginning of a work for a great
future, a work which will go on, perhaps, for tens of thousands
of years, in order that mankind may, even in the remote
future, come to know the truth of a real God . . ."

BIBLIOGRAPHY

Letters of Anton Tchehov to his family and Friends.   Chatto & Windus, 1920.

Anton Tchekhov.   Literary and theatrical Reminiscences.   G. Routledge & Sons, Ltd., 1927.

The Letters of Anton Pavlovitch Tchehov to Olga Leonardovna Knipper. Chatto & Windus, 1926.

The Plays of Tchehov. 2 volumes. Chatto & Windus, 1926.

The Tales of Tchehov. 13 volumes. Chatto & Windus, 1925.

My Life in Art, by Constantin Stanislavsky.   Geoffrey Bles, 1924.

The Life and Letters of Anton Tchekhov.   Cassell & Co., Ltd., 1925.

Anton Tchekhov's Note-books and Maxim Gorky's Reminiscences of Tchekhov, etc. The Hogarth Press, 1921.

Russia and the Russians in 1842, by J. G. Kohl, Esq. 2 volumes.   Henry Colburn, 1842.

Anton Chehov. A Critical Study, by William Gerhardi. Duckworth, 1923.

Index